THE STORY OF
NEGRO LEAGUE BASEBALL

THE STORY OF
NEGRO LEAGUE BASEBALL

WILLIAM BRASHLER

TICKNOR & FIELDS

BOOKS FOR YOUNG READERS

NEW YORK 1994

Published by Ticknor & Fields Books for Young Readers
A Houghton Mifflin company, 215 Park Avenue South,
New York, New York 10003

Manufactured in the United States of America
Book design by Jessica Shatan
The text of this book is set in 13 pt. Garamond #3
HOR 10 9 8 7 6 5 4 3 2 1

Library of Congress Cataloging-in-Publication Data
Brashler, William.
The story of Negro league baseball / by William Brashler
p. cm.
Includes bibliographic references and index.
ISBN 0-395-67169-8 (cl) — ISBN 0-395-69721-2 (pa)
1. Negro leagues—United States—History—Juvenile literature.
2. Crutchfield, Jimmie, 1910–1993—Juvenile literature. I. Title.
GV863.A1B72 1994
796.357'0973—dc20   93–36547   CIP   AC

Frontispiece: The 1887 Cuban Giants, black baseball's first great team, were not Cuban at all, but a collection of waiters from the Argyle Hotel on Long Island, New York. Some of the team's top players were pitchers Sol White and Shep Trusty, shortstop Abe Harrison, catcher Clarence Williams (sitting) and second baseman George Williams (standing).

For Bob and Cathy,
whose world is black and white and
all the colors in between.

ACKNOWLEDGMENTS

Much of the material in *The Story of Negro League Baseball* was obtained during personal interviews with former players and their wives and relatives. I first visited with James "Cool Papa" Bell and his wife, Clarabelle, in 1969, in their home in St. Louis, Missouri. Cool Papa directed me to Jimmie Crutchfield and his wife, Julia, Judy Johnson, Buck Leonard, Satchel Paige, Ted Page, Sam Streeter, and many others.

The stories and memories of these great ballplayers were used as background for my novel, *The Bingo Long Traveling All-Stars and Motor Kings,* which was published in 1973 and reissued in 1993. The novel was made into a movie starring James Earl Jones, Richard Pryor, and Billy Dee Williams in 1976. It is available on videocassette from Universal Pictures.

Over the years, I returned to Cool Papa and Jimmie Crutchfield and the others while researching a biography of Josh Gibson, the great and tragic Negro league legend. Others who helped in this effort were Jack Marshall, Vic Harris and his wife, Dorothy, David Malarcher, Ted "Double Duty" Radcliffe, Johnny Hayes, and Roy Campanella.

I also conducted dozens of interviews with other people too numerous to mention who were in some way involved with former Negro league players. All were helpful and insightful. Finally, I owe a debt of gratitude for the many hours spent with Bill Veeck and Mary-Frances Veeck, who knew everybody from Judge Kenesaw Mountain Landis to Satchel Paige and Larry Doby.

Many of the photographs in this book came from the scrapbooks of the Negro league players, such as Cool Papa Bell, Jimmie Crutchfield, and Jack Marshall. They were kind enough to let me make copies of priceless black-and-white photographs, clippings, and other mementos of their playing days. Jimmie Crutchfield also had a baseball signed by Josh Gibson, but he wisely would not let me borrow it.

Other photographs came from the collection of Dr. Lawrence Hogan of Union College, New Jersey. A curator and expert on the Negro leagues, Larry was executive producer of the superb documentary *Before You Can Say Jackie Robinson! Black Baseball in New Jersey and America in the Era of the Color Line, 1885–1950.* His help and insights were invaluable to me.

CONTENTS

INTRODUCTION:

THE MITE FROM MOBERLY

Jimmie Crutchfield was a little guy, a mite of a guy. Growing up as a country boy, he was always the shortest and skinniest of any of his friends. His hometown, a place called Moberly, Missouri, was in a farming and mining region. Jimmie's father was a coal miner. It was the 1920s. World War I had ended, and times were prosperous. Still, coal mines closed down often and finding steady work was hard. It was even harder for Jimmie's dad because he was black.

As for Jimmie, he had two loves: fishing and baseball. "We had a creek and a pond I could walk to. I loved to fish, and it helped put some food on the table," he said.

Baseball was a game he played barefoot in the Missouri fields on hot summer days. Sweat rolled down his face and dust blew in his eyes, but the heat and dust never bothered him. He loved to play baseball, and he played it well. He ran like a rabbit. He hit the ball—sometimes they had no ball and played with rocks or crushed milk cans—in hard line drives. He caught anything he could get close to. He was so good that people went out of their way to watch him.

"At the end of the day," Jimmie Crutchfield said, "the coal miners would come in from the mines, and they would gather around to watch us play. It was one of the highlights of the day."

Yet he was *small*. At fourteen, Jimmie was just over five feet tall and weighed only 100 pounds. With his impish smile he always looked younger than he was. People said, "Crutch"—for that was his nickname—"you'll never make it against the big guys."

Hearing that, Crutchfield played even harder, and soon he was the top performer on any team he joined. He had a quick bat, and he slashed the ball to all fields. If a pitcher gave him a step, he stole a base. He skittered like a bug in the outfield. He was smart, heads-up, and tougher than any player his size had a right to be.

When he was eighteen—now five feet seven inches and weighing 138 pounds—he met an old ballplayer named Bill Gatewood. Gatewood had played professional baseball, and he knew talent when he saw it. He was one of the first people to tell Crutchfield that he was not too small, that he was a real player.

"I like the way you play ball, Crutch," Gatewood said.

In 1930, at age twenty, Crutchfield was sent by Gatewood to Birmingham, Alabama, where he joined the Black Barons, one of the strong professional teams in Negro baseball. Even then, the owner took one look at him and wanted to send him back to Moberly because he was so small. "When you face those big pitchers in Chicago and St. Louis and Kansas City," the owner said, "they'll knock that bat right out of your hands!"

The Pittsburgh Crawfords, featuring young outfielder Jimmie Crutchfield. The 1932 team was made up of many Negro league all-stars. Kneeling (left to right): Sam Streeter, Chester Williams, Harry Williams, Harry "Tincan" Kincannon, Henry Spearman, Jimmie Crutchfield, Bobby Williams, Ted "Double Duty" Radcliffe. Standing (left to right): owner Gus Greenlee, T. Jones, L. D. Livingston, Satchel Paige, Josh Gibson, Roy Williams, Walter "Rev" Cannady, Bill Perkins, Oscar Charleston, club secretary John Clark.

Crutchfield smiled. He had heard that before. He put on the cap of the Birmingham Black Barons—it had three *B*s on the front—and was ready to go. Five years later, having moved from the Barons to a team called the Pittsburgh [Pennsylvania] Crawfords, Jimmie Crutchfield was to show the world just how far he had come.

The year was 1935, and America's president was Franklin Delano Roosevelt. Times were hard, so hard that the era was called the Great

Depression. Jobs were scarce, and many people moved from city to city looking for work. Still, a crowd of twenty-five thousand men and women, most of them black, came out one warm August afternoon to Chicago's Comiskey Park to see a baseball game.

What a game it was! Maybe the best ever, some people said. The teams were the East and West All-Stars, the best players from the Negro baseball leagues, the other major leagues. They were all blacks—called Negroes then—and Latinos, the aces of the America's Negro baseball leagues.

There were players like the tall, skinny, fire-balling pitcher named Leroy Paige. As a boy he had worked carrying satchels—suitcases—for railroad passengers, so he was nicknamed Satchel Paige.

There was a lightning-quick outfielder named James "Cool Papa" Bell who was so fast, people said, that he could turn out the light and jump into bed before the room got dark.

There was a strong, stocky slugger named Josh Gibson who, the story goes, once hit a ball out of sight in a stadium in Pittsburgh. The next day he was playing in Altoona, Pennsylvania, when a ball fell out of the sky and landed in an outfielder's glove. The umpire ran over to Gibson and yelled, "You're out! Yesterday in Pittsburgh!"

There were many others: players with nicknames like Mule and Double Duty and Turkey and Big Florida, all remarkable hitters and pitchers and fielders.

And among them was the Mite from Moberly, Jimmie Crutchfield. Even though he had not grown nor gained much weight, Crutch had become a star among these stars, a bug of an outfielder, and a dangerous hitter, the equal of giants like Paige, Bell, and Gibson.

As he stood on the lush green grass of the outfield in Comiskey Park, a major league stadium that had been borrowed by the Negro leagues for this special game, Crutch could hardly believe that he was there. This great stadium, thousands of people in the stands, his pressed Crawfords uniform: how far it was from the hot, weedy fields of Moberly, Missouri. "It was like a dream to me," he said.

The game began with plenty of hits and runs. The East team jumped ahead 4–0 after five innings, only to see the West, Crutchfield's squad, tie it 4–4 after seven innings. In the ninth inning, however, the East put men on base and their power-hitting catcher, Biz Mackey, came to the plate. Mackey whacked a drive to center field that looked like nobody could get to it. Except that Jimmie Crutchfield was out there.

Crutchfield took off, his little legs churning, the ball screaming away from him. In seconds, however, he got to the ball just before it flew over his head. He leaped like a jumping spider, he extended his *bare* hand, and he got it! He snapped the ball out of the air—it stung but Crutchfield didn't mind—and Mackey was out. Mackey could only kick the dirt in disgust. Crutchfield's West team was still alive, and when Jimmie got back to the dugout he was mobbed by teammates almost twice his size. Many of them said they had never seen a better catch by anyone anywhere.

In the eleventh inning, one of Crutchfield's teammates finally won the game for the West with a long, three-run home run. Thousands of fans jumped onto the field to celebrate. Years later they would remember that home run and other good hits. But the play they would crow about was that bare-handed catch by that little guy, Crutchfield.

For the rest of his life Crutch would remember that catch, and a great smile would break out on his face. "Oh, I'll never forget that," he would say.

There is, however, one sad thing about that exciting game and the performances of players like Jimmie Crutchfield: most people in the United States in 1935 had not even heard about them. The East-West All-Star game was played by black and brown men in a time when baseball in America was a divided, segregated sport. White men played for good salaries in major league stadiums. Black and brown men played for almost nothing in any ballpark that would have them.

White men wore fresh, clean uniforms that were laundered for them by clubhouse attendants. Black men wore the same uniform over and over again and washed it themselves when they could. White men traveled to scheduled games in reserved passenger trains and stayed in large hotels. Black men rode in rickety buses or overloaded cars and had to stay in rooming houses or "Negro" motels. White men ate in the best restaurants. Black men were never certain if a restaurant would serve them or not.

The major leagues were populated by famous, rich stars like Babe Ruth and Dizzy Dean and Hank Greenberg. Their games were broadcast on radio and reported in every newspaper in the country. No black or Latino player could challenge them for their jobs. Major league owners had agreed many years earlier not to sign nonwhite players, and that ban held for almost fifty years.

No matter how good they were, no matter that they could stroke baseballs far into the stands of major league ballparks or catch line drives with their bare hands, the stars of Negro baseball were confined to their own leagues and mostly to their own fans. Players like Jimmie Crutchfield, Satchel Paige, Cool Papa Bell, and Josh Gibson—men who played the game as well as the Hank Aarons, Reggie Jacksons, and Kirby Pucketts who followed them decades later—were largely unknown and unappreciated by white baseball fans.

And yet the baseball they played was remarkable. Some of their teams were among the best in baseball history. The experiences they had—even the hard times—were unforgettable. Black ballplayers made history, and it was history more exciting and eventful than almost any other in baseball.

The color line in professional baseball was broken in 1945 when Jackie Robinson signed with the Brooklyn Dodgers. He soon became a major league star. "Quicker than you can say Jackie Robinson" was a common saying, because Robinson was so fast and so good. He was a pioneer, and a hero to black people. But Robinson and the other nonwhite players that followed him into the major leagues owed a debt to those many dark-skinned players who never had the chance. Players like Jimmie Crutchfield.

"I was very happy for Jackie," said Crutchfield. "I knew he would make it. But we could play, too. We knew that. Sometimes when I look back, it's very tough to take."

Jimmie Crutchfield, the Mite from Moberly, died on March 31, 1993, at the age of eighty-three.

Negro league baseball, his game and a game where only the ball was white, was a bitter but remarkable treasure. Here is its story.

IN THE BEGINNING:

A GAME OF COLOR

Before there was a light bulb or an automobile, there was baseball. Before the Civil War or Jesse James and Wyatt Earp, there was baseball. The common belief is that the game was created in 1839 in Cooperstown, New York, by General Abner Doubleday. Major league baseball's Hall of Fame is in Cooperstown. But those claims for Doubleday and Cooperstown as the nurse and cradle of baseball may not be altogether true.

The first recorded baseball game in America was played on June 19, 1846, in Hoboken, New Jersey. It was the idea of Alexander J. Cartright, whose New York Knickerbockers played a team called the New York Nine. Cartright, not Doubleday, should be considered the father of modern baseball. His team, by the way, lost 23–1.

Yet games like baseball were played in Europe long before America was settled, and running games using sticks and balls were played in ancient Egypt and Greece. Trying to pinpoint who invented baseball, wrote researcher Dr. Harold Seymour, is like "trying to locate the discoverer of fire."

It is certain, however, that although baseball has long been one of America's favorite sports, baseball is not an American creation. The English, for example, had a popular game called "rounders." It was played on a field with four posts or stones placed in a diamond-shaped pattern. The pitcher was called a "feeder" and the batter was called a "striker," and the game was played much like baseball is today.

When colonists came to the so-called New World, they brought their old-world games with them. In 1762, an English book of games called *A Little Pretty Pocket-Book* was republished in New York, and it included rules and drawings of what was called "base-ball." During the Revolutionary War, an American soldier at Valley Forge wrote about playing a game of "base" on the campground.

In the nineteenth century, baseball was played in many ways in all parts of society. Young white men from well-to-do families played the game on prep school teams in grassy fields. Slaves played in pastures with sticks or broomsticks and balls made of cotton or of boiled chicken feathers and tightly wrapped with cloth. Sometimes players wound twine tightly into a ball and wrapped a cloth around it.

The game then was called "towne ball," and was played by different sets of rules. There was no official distance between home plate and the pitcher's mound, nor between the bases. The pitcher threw the ball underhand. A runner could be put out by "plugging" or "soaking" him, which meant hitting him with a thrown ball.

It was Alexander J. Cartright who put the bases ninety feet

apart, as they are today. He also established an umpire, three outs
for each side, and tagging a runner out instead of throwing the ball
at him. But at that time the pitcher stood only fifty feet away from
home plate, and he did not have to stand on a pitching rubber. He
could move around in a five-by-four-foot area. Not until 1893,
almost fifty years later, was the pitcher's mound put sixty feet six
inches from home plate, where it remains today.

Baseball started to grow as an organized sport in the late nineteenth century. America was still a very rural country, and baseball
was the perfect pickup game for any open pasture. Most small
towns and neighborhoods had teams—boys' and men's teams,
girls' and women's teams, church teams. There were factory teams,
even prison teams. They competed in summer leagues and exhibition play wherever possible.

By 1871, when the country was rebuilding itself after the
ravages of the Civil War, several professional baseball leagues were
formed, most of them in the Eastern, more populated part of the
country. The United States' first major professional league, called
the National League, was formed in 1876 by William Hulbert,
owner of the Chicago White Stockings. There were eight teams:
Boston, Chicago, Cincinnati (Ohio), St. Louis (Missouri), Hart-
ford (Connecticut), New York, Philadelphia, and Louisville
(Kentucky).

The best players from all over the country were drawn to these
teams. They were brawny, tough men, many of them wearing fat,
handlebar mustaches. They played with thick wooden bats and
heavy, scuffed leather balls. They fielded the ball bare-handed or
with leather mitts that were not much thicker than winter gloves.
They had no helmets, and the catcher wore only a thin chest pad
and a puny wire mask.

The games these men played were mean, rugged affairs, with many fistfights and arguments. Most players and coaches chewed fat chaws of tobacco, and they often spat the juice on the ball or at each other. Pitchers threw spitballs that jumped and curved all over the place. If a batter stood too close to the plate, a pitcher threw a hard fastball at his head, something called a "knockdown" pitch.

Although people loved to watch baseball and the sport was becoming "America's pastime," it was not yet considered a glamorous or noble pursuit. The pay was low, many players were hard drinkers and bullies, and teams often folded or disbanded overnight. When Casey Stengel, who began his baseball career playing on sandlot teams in Kansas City and later became a famous manager, told his parents in 1910 that he was quitting dental school to play baseball, they were very upset. It was not the kind of thing respectable parents wanted a son to do.

One of the National League's first stars was Adrian "Cap" Anson, a tough first baseman from Iowa who played for William Hulbert's Chicago White Stockings from 1876 to 1897. He later managed and became part owner of the team, and his influence on all of professional baseball in its early years was very great. Unfortunately, Anson also played a personal role in the creation of the sport's greatest injustice.

In the late nineteenth century, America was struggling with the issue of blacks and their place in society. The Civil War and the Emancipation Proclamation made them free, but discrimination and the effects of years of slavery were still a part of American life. Many of the early professional baseball associations barred Negroes from their teams; others, however, allowed players of all colors.

As late as 1885, an estimated sixty black players—they were called "colored" then—could be found on minor league teams.

Moses Fleetwood "Fleet" Walker played for Toledo in 1884 and is considered the first black in the major leagues. Before an 1884 exhibition game with the Toledo club, Cap Anson of the Chicago White Stockings threatened to take his team off the field if Walker played. Walker played anyway, and the game went on.

These teams were in leagues just below the National League, and their best players usually went up to the parent league.

One of the first black minor league players was John W. "Bud" Fowler, an infielder from New York, who played from 1872 until 1897. Fowler could play almost any position. He was such a fast runner that he delighted crowds by racing against roller skaters. Teams formed and folded quickly, so Fowler traveled all over the country, playing for any squad that would give him a job.

The black player considered the first to play major league baseball was Moses Fleetwood "Fleet" Walker, a tall, light-skinned catcher from Ohio. Walker was well educated. He had attended Oberlin College and the University of Michigan, and played baseball at both places before joining Toledo in 1884, in the Major League American Association.

His younger brother, Weldy Walker, also played, and followed

Fleet onto the Toledo roster later in the year. The response from white players and fans to the Walkers was generally good. The hometown fans appreciated their fine play and hustle. When the team traveled to some Southern towns, though, the Walkers were jeered at and ridiculed. Racist thugs sent threatening letters to the team warning that Fleet Walker would be mobbed if he appeared on the field.

Of the early black pioneers, Frank Grant was one of the best players. He also received some of the roughest treatment, and it came not just from fans, but from his fellow players. As a second baseman, he covered the bag on force-outs or steal attempts. Many opposing runners went out of their way to kick Grant with their spikes. It got so bad that Grant fashioned crude shin guards out of wood to protect himself. He later switched to the outfield to avoid having to deal with runners.

It was amazing that Grant could play at all with such treatment. When he was hitting, white pitchers often threw at his head. Still, Grant led his team, the Buffalo [New York] Bisons, in hitting during the 1888 season.

Overall, black players during those early years found it rough going. They were often yelled at by fans or opponents who used slurs like "niggers," "coons," or "darkies." Some of their white teammates refused to pose with them for team photographs. Still, blacks were not kept off white teams. George Stovey, a left-handed pitcher from Canada; Frank Grant, an infielder; Robert Higgins, a pitcher; Sol White, an infielder; and several others appeared on various rosters.

That was to change largely because of Cap Anson. In July 1887, Anson, the superstar of the Chicago White Stockings, was scheduled to lead his team against the Newark [New Jersey] Little

Frank Grant (front row, second from right), the only black on the Buffalo Bisons in the 1880s. Though small—five feet seven inches and 155 pounds—Grant was a top slugger in the International Professional League.

Giants. The game was an exhibition, which means it was not part of league play. Back then it was common for big leaguers to play games against local teams in order to make extra money. There was no television, so these games were the only times many fans could see the stars they read about in the sports pages.

Like any other sport, baseball needed superstars like Cap Anson to increase its popularity, and Anson was so famous that wherever he went, thousands of people would pay to see him play. Big stars like Anson could do almost anything they wanted to do. Anson could decide whom he would and would not play, and often that meant he would not compete against black players.

On the eve of the game between Anson's White Stockings and the Little Giants of Newark, everybody looked forward to the contest between Anson and George Stovey, the Little Giants' best pitcher, who was black. It was not to be. According to the Newark newspaper, Stovey did not pitch because he was sick. The game was played without him—Newark still won—but a year later it was revealed that Anson had refused to put his team on the field if Stovey was allowed to play. The black pitcher was kept out against his will so that the game would not be forfeited.

Many people point to Cap Anson's stand against blacks as a major turning point in baseball's racial history. He was an important star—one of the most famous players in the game before Ty Cobb and Babe Ruth. He made no secret of his ill feelings toward players with black or brown skin, and he was big enough to make a strong player like George Stovey suddenly get "sick" and sit out a game.

Still, Anson did not do it alone. Historians agree that in professional baseball's early days, the majority of its white players opposed integrated teams. As in the rest of society, black Americans were not guaranteed equality on the baseball field. As the twentieth century approached, the future did not look good for George Stovey, Frank Grant, and the many other superb but dark-skinned ballplayers.

At the same time, however, blacks were forming their own teams. Many of these were made up of men who worked together, or who belonged to the same church, social club, or neighborhood.

Adrian "Cap" Anson of the Chicago
White Stockings, as he appeared in the
1880s.

One of the first and most important black baseball squads was formed in the summer of 1885 by a group of waiters who worked at the Argyle Hotel in Babylon, New York. The Argyle was a popular summer resort, and the team of black waiters, called the Athletics, added to the guests' entertainment.

That fall the Athletics stayed together and went on the road to play all comers. When they did so, however, the team changed its name to the Cuban Giants. The players believed that white fans would be more attracted to a team of foreign players than to a group of black American hotel waiters. On the field, they even spoke in nonsense words or gibberish to persuade the fans that they were foreigners. Then, and for many years to come, white Americans accepted foreigners of different colors before they accepted black Americans.

Negro league players often told the story, which few of them found funny, of the white manager who was bothered by a black teenager who wanted to play on his team. The manager told the young man again and again that he wasn't good enough. The real reason, of course, was his color. But the black kid would not quit pestering the manager and, finally, during a game in which the opposing team had their all-star pitcher on the mound, the manager told the teenager to get a bat and go up to the plate. The young man did, and on the first pitch he clouted a long drive against the fence. As the kid was rounding second base and heading into third for a triple, the manager yelled out, "Look at that *Cuban* run!"

The Cuban Giants played well against professional and college teams and soon made a name for themselves. Many fine black players signed with the team, but they did so for less money than they would have gotten from white teams. The Cubans paid players between twelve and eighteen dollars a week, not even half of what white teams paid their players. No matter how much success black players found with these teams, the low pay was a bitter pill to take. The best black players—Bud Fowler, George Stovey, and others—still sought out any higher-paying white team that would sign them.

By the 1890s, good black teams were playing all over the country. Besides the Cuban Giants, there were the New York Cuban X Giants, the New York Gorhams, the New Orleans [Louisiana] Pinchbacks, two Philadelphia teams called the Orions and the Mutuals, the Chicago Unions, and several others. Many of these teams made money by going on the road or "barnstorming," which meant they played almost any opponent for whatever money the promoters could raise. With games in Western states and in Florida, the Cuban Giants played all year round.

Every team was eager to play the best white teams, especially major league teams or teams with major league players on them. (At that time, and for many years after, major league players were allowed to play with other teams in exhibition games.) To the black teams, exhibition games were a chance to show that they were as good as or better than the white teams. Many black teams, especially the Cuban Giants, showed just that. Their record against white teams was so good that many white squads refused to play them for fear of being beaten and embarrassed.

At the same time as these black teams formed and signed more and more black- and brown-skinned players, more and more white professional teams were no longer signing black players. By 1900, no blacks were playing on white teams, and it looked like none ever would again. Some leagues had written bylaws prohibiting nonwhite players, but most of them, particularly the major leagues, had an informal rule that barred blacks and Latinos. This kind of rule came to be known as a "gentleman's agreement," something which was not written down, but which was based on "honor." But there was no honor in this unfair pact.

Keeping blacks off white professional baseball teams was a grave symbol of race relations in America at the time. Thirty-five years after the Civil War had ended slavery, blacks were still being denied basic opportunities. Baseball was the country's favorite game; everybody watched and played it. Yet it was a game with a color line: blacks and whites could not be teammates. And nobody dared to cross that line.

JIM CROW COMES
TO BASEBALL

Before television or radio, people enjoyed live entertainment in the form of vaudeville and minstrel shows. Traveling singers, dancers, and comedians appeared onstage at local theaters. The singing was lighthearted, and the comedy frequently involved wild slapstick routines in which the actors hit one another on the head with rubber hammers and heavy balloons called pig bladders. In minstrel shows, the performers were often white men who dressed up in ridiculous costumes and painted their faces black to pretend to be Negroes.

In 1828, a minstrel show performer named Thomas Dartmouth "Daddy" Rice created a blackface routine called "Jump Jim Crow." It became extremely popular and was imitated by minstrel-show actors all over the country. "Jim Crow," a nickname for the black bird, soon became a commonly known and insulting term used for blacks.

After the Civil War ended in 1865, many states passed laws that separated whites from blacks, or "persons of color." These were called segregation laws, and became known as Jim Crow laws. They forbade blacks to go to white schools, eat in white restaurants, or play in white parks. Blacks and whites could not sit together in theaters or on buses and trains. Even public drinking fountains were designated as "white" or "colored." By 1900, Jim Crow was showing his cruel face everywhere in America—including the baseball diamond.

The beginning of the twentieth century saw major league baseball becoming more and more popular. Star players like Pittsburgh's Honus Wagner, a pure hitter who could play almost any position; Cy Young, one of the greatest pitchers who ever lived; and Napoleon "Nap" Lajoie, a superb second baseman, were heroes to fans.

Major league baseball was also expanding. In 1901, the National League was challenged by the new American League. To stock its rosters, the new teams raided the National League for talent. The Chicago National League club, Cap Anson's team, had been known as the White Stockings. When the team lost so many veteran players to the American League raiders, they had to replace them with new young players. Sportswriters called the new ballplayers "cubs." The name stuck; the White Stockings became the Chicago Cubs.

Each new club desperately needed talent, because fans wanted a winning team, but none of them looked to black teams for help. Almost none, that is. In 1901, John J. "Muggsy" McGraw, a former star player who was to become one of baseball's best managers, was managing the new Baltimore team in the American League. He needed players, and he decided he wanted to sign one

Charlie or Tokohama? Charlie Grant, a light-skinned black infielder for the 1901 Columbia Giants, attracted the interest of New York Giants manager John McGraw. McGraw wanted to rename Grant "Tokohama" and put him into the major leagues as an American Indian. The ploy did not work.

named Charlie Grant. Grant was working as a bellboy in the hotel where McGraw was staying. During his off-hours, Grant and the other hotel employees played baseball, and John McGraw saw that Grant was a good second baseman. He was also black. A year earlier he had played for a Negro team called the Chicago Columbia Giants.

McGraw knew of the unwritten ban on black players, yet he also knew that players of lighter colors were accepted. (The Cubans Armando Marsans and Rafael Almeida played for Cincinnati beginning with the 1911 season.) The story goes that McGraw was looking at a map in the hotel one day, trying to figure out how to sign Charlie Grant. Grant was light-skinned and he had wavy hair. McGraw suddenly spotted a creek named Tokohama and said, "That's going to be your name from now on, Chief Tokohama, and you're a full-blooded Cherokee Indian."

McGraw and Grant tried to add "Tokohama" to the Orioles roster, but the trick was soon discovered. When the Orioles played Chicago in an exhibition, black fans turned out to celebrate Grant's appearance. They even gave him "Indian" presents, such as an alligator-skin wallet. Charles Comiskey, the owner of the Chicago White Sox, objected angrily: "Somebody told me that the Cherokee of McGraw's is really Grant, the crack Negro second baseman fixed up with war paint and a bunch of feathers."

By the end of spring training that year, the objection to Grant's playing with the Orioles was too strong. McGraw gave up. Charlie Grant never played in the major leagues.

Just as the white leagues were adding more teams after the year 1900, Negro teams also became more numerous. The best new teams formed in Northern big cities like New York, Philadelphia, and Chicago. Most of these teams were "semi-professional": the players held regular jobs and played baseball only part-time. Often they toured the country and drew large crowds.

The best of the new teams included New York's Lincoln Giants, the Chicago Union Giants, the Philadelphia Giants, the Homestead Grays (which came out of a steel town near Pittsburgh), the Hilldale club from Pennsylvania, the Bacharach Giants from Atlantic City (New Jersey), and Indiana's Indianapolis ABC's. Many teams took the name Giants because the major league New York Giants was one of the best of the early white professional teams.

There was not yet an established Negro league, so these teams were independents. The teams that stayed together at this time did so because of strong owners. Frank Leland of Chicago formed both the Union Giants and the Leland Giants teams, and kept them going for years. Nat C. Strong ran the New York Lincoln Giants. The best teams played against one another or against any white team that would give them a game. Often they had a series of games and the winner would be declared the champion of the region.

Most players did not have contracts, or if they did, the agreements were not much more than a handshake. That meant players could jump from team to team if they wanted to make a few extra dollars. A player might perform for a Chicago club on Saturday and play on Sunday in Gary, Indiana, for a different team. Even white, major league players sometimes played in exhibition games for extra money, but these players had contracts which did not permit them to do this. When they played exhibition ball, they used different names so their team owners would not find out.

Many fans wanted to see the best black teams, such as the Lincoln Giants or the Chicago Union Giants, play against the best white teams. Sportswriters in black newspapers and the owners of black teams often called for a real World Series: white champions versus black champions. A black-white World Series never took place, but some major league squads, such as the Chicago Cubs, played against Negro league teams and teams made up of black all-stars. The games were usually very close contests.

In 1910, for example, the Detroit Tigers, led by the famous Ty Cobb, played twelve games against a team made up of black stars. The Tigers won seven, lost four, and tied one. In 1915 major league teams played eight exhibition games against black teams. The black teams won four; the big-league teams won four.

These exhibition games made it plain to most baseball fans that many black players were equal in skill to white major leaguers. Still, the major league color line was not broken. No black players, not even the superstars, ever held the dimmest hope of playing in the white leagues.

The early twentieth century saw an important turning point in black American history. Blacks began what became known as the Great Migration. They moved in huge numbers from the South to the North. Jim Crow laws in the South made blacks feel that slavery had been abolished in name but not as a practice. Many Southern blacks continued to work for low wages on farms and lived in shacks outside of town.

At this time, industry in the Northern states was expanding. Factories were making steel, automobiles, and other modern products. They needed workers no matter what color their skin might be. In the large cities there were black newspapers, such as the *Chicago Defender,* the *New York Amsterdam News,* and the *Pittsburgh Courier.* These newspapers urged Southern blacks to come north.

One way these newspapers encouraged blacks to move was by showing how bad life was in the South. They wrote disturbing stories about lynchings. In a lynching, a black, often a teenage boy, was kidnapped and hanged by a white gang for something he supposedly did wrong. The papers ran terrible photographs and kept count of lynchings. *Come north where life is better,* wrote the newspapers. *It may not be perfect, but it is better.* In some areas of the South, officials tried to stop the sale of the papers to keep their message out of the hands of their black citizens, but by and large the papers continued to be distributed.

Thousands of black families packed up everything they owned and moved north. Railway lines set up direct routes from Southern cities to Chicago, Pittsburgh, Cleveland, New York City, and other cities. Detroit, for example, became a great automobile center, and jobs in the auto plants lured black workers. In 1917, sixty-five thousand blacks came to Chicago alone. Most moved into crowded black communities, where there was a new spirit and a new freedom to black life.

Negro baseball grew right along with the black population. Black players came north to play on the top teams. Whole teams came north. The Duval Giants of Jacksonville, Florida, became the Bacharach Giants of Atlantic City, New Jersey. Some games drew crowds of as many as ten thousand people. Some of the best players became well-known stars. They were written about in the black newspapers, and black fans came out to see them just as white fans followed their stars.

Not as much is known of these early players as of the later stars. Black newspapers did not report the games in detail like they would years later. White newspapers, of course, did not report the games at all. Some of the early stars were great athletes, however, and their play was talked about long after they were dead. They were the true pioneers of black baseball and their stories deserve to be remembered.

One of the first great players was the pitcher Andrew "Rube" Foster. At six feet four inches and 200 pounds, with muscular arms and a thick neck, Foster could throw a ball past most hitters. He was born in 1879 in Calvert, Texas, where his father was a minister. In the eighth grade he left school to play baseball full-time. At seventeen he was the ace pitcher for a touring ball club called the Waco [Texas] Yellow Jackets. He threw sidearm, with his arm dipping low in what is called a "submarine" pitch: the ball came toward the outside of the plate and dipped across it.

Foster came north in 1902 to play for the Chicago Union

Giants, and soon had a reputation for being wild and unruly. One teammate said Foster actually packed his Texas pistol wherever he went. But Foster's pitching talent soon prevailed. In 1903 he joined the Cuban X Giants and led them against the Philadelphia Giants, a team that called itself the World's Colored Champions. The Cuban X Giants challenged that claim and they beat the Philly club five times in a seven-game series. Foster was the winning pitcher in four of the five victories.

That same year Foster outhurled a top white major leaguer named Rube Waddell of the Philadelphia Athletics. From then on Andrew Foster was "Rube" Foster, a pitcher as good as any alive.

In 1907 Foster went back to Chicago and played for a strong team called the Leland Giants. Unhappy with the low pay he and his teammates received, he dickered with the owner for a higher fee. That was the first sign that Rube Foster was a player with a sharp mind as well as a good arm.

While Foster dominated the pitching mound, nobody was more popular as a fielder and hitter than John Henry "Pop" Lloyd. A tall, slick shortstop, Lloyd was a left-handed hitter who could hit anything and hit it far. He not only batted a consistent .400 but he was usually the number-four hitter—the clean-up hitter who could "clean" the bases with a grand slam homer. Those who saw Lloyd play called him one of the greatest black players of his day—and any day.

Like many other black players, Lloyd was raised in the South. He was born in 1884 in Palatka, Florida. His father died when Lloyd was a baby, and his grandmother raised him. He dropped out of school at age thirteen and worked odd jobs, but soon he worked only at baseball. In 1906 he starred for the Cuban X Giants in Philadelphia. From then on, he played for the team that paid him

Rube Foster and the 1906 Philadelphia Giants called themselves World's Champions because they beat the Cuban X Giants, who had called themselves World's Champions the year before. Foster (standing, second from right) was the star pitcher both years, first for the Cuban X Giants and then for Philadelphia.

the most. "Wherever the money was, that's where I was," he used to say.

In his prime—between 1910 and 1920—Lloyd played for the Leland Giants in Chicago, the Lincoln Giants in New York, and the Chicago American Giants. The American Giants paid him $250 a month, a salary no other black player could match.

Besides his great play, Lloyd was loved by the fans because of his easy smile and positive attitude. He possessed a wide, confident grin, and he often patted his fellow players on the back. Yet he

John Henry Lloyd and friends. The 1912 New York Lincoln Giants boasted many of the greatest black stars of all time. Shortstop John Henry Lloyd (standing, center) was the best player of his era. Pitchers Smokey Joe Williams and Dick "Cannonball" Redding (sitting, respectively, third and fourth from left) had the best arms in the game. Other greats were catcher Louis "Top" Santop (sitting, second from left) and outfielder Spotswood "Spot" Poles (standing, far right).

played hard. One opponent called him the "Dr. Jekyll and Mr. Hyde of baseball," after the famous story of a man with two personalities, one fierce and one friendly.

Later in his career, Lloyd was a player-manager, usually playing first base. He got the nickname Pop because he was fatherly toward young players. He played with good black teams until he was forty-seven years old, and even then, the younger players admired his ability.

Like other black players, Pop Lloyd was compared to the

famous white major leaguers of the time. He was called "the black Honus Wagner," after the fine Pittsburgh Pirate shortstop. Baseball experts of his day rated Wagner "the best all-round ballplayer who ever lived," but when a sportswriter asked Wagner himself who he thought was the best player, he answered, "If you mean in all baseball, organized or unorganized, the answer would have to be a colored man named John Henry Lloyd."

Another top player of this era was Joe Williams, a pitcher who rivaled Rube Foster in speed and ability. A Texan, he was called Smokey Joe or Cyclone Joe. Williams was tall—about six feet six inches—and powerfully graceful, with bronze skin and a thin, handsome face. His mother was part Indian, and people said Williams looked like an Indian warrior.

Williams's right arm was amazing. He threw straight over-hand. Batters said the ball looked the size of a pea when it came in, and one opponent added that Joe was so tall, his ball looked as if it was "coming off a mountaintop."

Born in 1886, he joined the San Antonio Broncos, a black semi-professional team, at the age of fourteen. The Williams family moved to Chicago in 1901, where many teams in the city's semi-professional leagues wanted Joe to pitch for them. Often he was the only black player on the team. Later, in his best years, Williams played for the top Negro teams, including the Leland Giants, the Lincoln Giants, and the Homestead Grays.

Williams's speed made him a strikeout pitcher. He often fanned as many as twenty batters a game. In 1914, his best season, Williams won forty-one and lost only three games for the Chicago American Giants. In 1915, while playing for the Lincoln Giants, he beat the National League champion Philadelphia Phillies, 1–0.

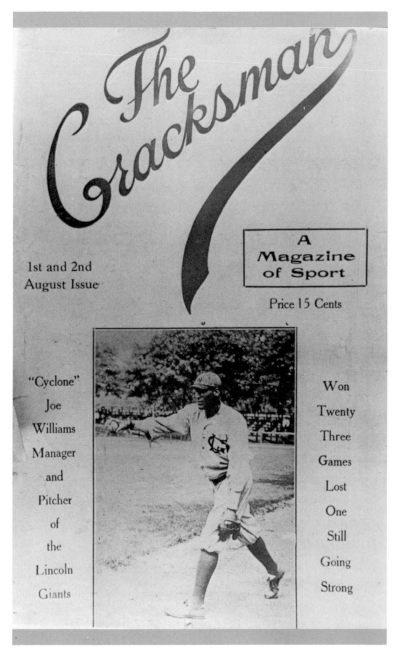

Joe Williams. Handsome, lean, with a hard stare or a slight smile, Williams was known as Cyclone Joe or Smokey Joe. Williams is shown here on the cover of The Cracksman, *a sports magazine, in 1921, when he starred for the New York Lincoln Giants.*

In the ninth inning he struck out the side with nine straight strikes.

Although he threw hard, Williams pitched with a look of calm on his face. Sometimes he even smiled slightly when men got on base against him. His was the smile of pure confidence. When he lost some of his speed, he changed his pitching style. He threw sidearm and offered a curve that broke sharply down. He even developed a knuckleball, the pitch where the ball is gripped by the knuckles and thrown so slowly that it seems to flutter in the air like a butterfly.

There were several other outstanding players on the early black teams.

Oscar Charleston was a thick-chested, lightning-fast outfielder and a solid hitter. In the outfield, he often played close in behind second base, but he could outrun any ball hit over his head. As he grew older and heavier, he moved to first base. Charleston batted left-handed. His barrel chest and skinny legs reminded people of Babe Ruth's.

Charleston began his career with the Indianapolis ABC's in 1915. He went on to play for and manage many teams until 1950. When on tour, his teammates said, he often hit a home run every night. Later, as a manager, he was a stern coach who would not allow any fooling around. Old-time black players once voted Charleston the best black player ever.

Wilbur "Bullet" or "Bullet Joe" Rogan was another fireballing pitcher, and an all-around player too. He often pitched the first game of a doubleheader and played other positions in the second game. His opponents said Bullet Joe had the fastest pitch in baseball. He pitched mainly for the Kansas City Monarchs between 1919 and 1938. Like most pitchers of his day, he threw nine or

Oscar the Great. A pick on everybody's all-time Negro league all-star team, Oscar Charleston was a speedy outfielder who often played just behind second base, and a left-handed hitter who could crush the ball. As he got older and fatter, he played first base and hit Babe Ruth–style home runs.

more innings every game. He also was a good hitter.

One of the top sluggers was Louis "Top" Santop, who played from 1909 to 1926. Soon after Babe Ruth's home runs made him baseball's greatest star, Santop was called the "black Babe Ruth." A catcher for the New York Lincoln Giants and Philadelphia's Hilldale team, Santop whacked long home runs at a time when the ball was very heavy or "dead." Like Ruth, he hit left-handed. Sometimes Top pointed his finger to the stands, to say he was going to hit a home run—something Babe Ruth also did, many years later.

"Cannonball" Dick Redding got his nickname because of his very powerful fastball. He was a right-handed pitcher for the New

York Lincoln Giants and many other teams from 1911 to 1938. In 1912 he had a record of forty-three wins and twelve losses for the Lincoln Giants. Redding often played against major-leaguers and struck them out as often as he did his black opponents. Many old-timers put him among the best pitchers of all time. He sometimes stood on one leg and turned his back to the batter for a second or two before he fired the ball.

Another ace player on the Chicago American Giants was David "Gentleman Dave" Malarcher. He received that nickname because he had a soft, high-pitched voice and he never played unfairly. As a third baseman, he gobbled up anything hit near him. He was a fast runner who could hit left- or right-handed for a high average. Born in Louisiana in 1894, Malarcher was a player-manager from 1916 to 1934. People not only admired his ability, but he was one of the most well-liked players in black baseball.

Spotswood "Spot" Poles was called the "black Ty Cobb" after the fierce Detroit Tigers superstar. Poles played center field for the New York Lincoln Giants and other teams from 1909 to 1923. His speed made him a great lead-off hitter and base-stealer. His batting average in 1911 for the Lincoln Giants was .440.

These and other early black stars played for many top teams, but no team was better than the Chicago American Giants. The squad was formed in 1911 by Rube Foster, still a star pitcher at the time. Foster, in partnership with a white Chicago businessman named John Schorling, became co-owner, manager, and player for the American Giants. The team soon became known as "Rube Foster's Giants."

The American Giants played other black teams in Chicago and white semi-professional teams. Foster leased a ballpark on Chicago's South Side and built grandstands that would hold 9000 fans. Foster paid his players well and drew some of the biggest names in the game at that time. His 1914 Giants included Smokey Joe Williams and John Henry Lloyd. Later Foster added such stars as Oscar Charleston, Dick Redding, and Louis Santop. He made these good players play hard. And he made them play fast.

The American Giants were known for speed. People called them a team of racehorses. Foster, as a manager on the field, or later, managing the team from the stands while smoking a big cigar, loved to have his players bunt the ball with men on base. He called it the hit-and-run bunt. When it succeeded, a fast runner on first often advanced two bases instead of one, and if an infielder threw wildly, the runner might score. Some people think Foster's American Giant teams were the greatest black squads that ever played.

Foster equipped the team with as many as five sets of uniforms, which was remarkable in those times because black teams often lacked the money for even one complete set. Players came to games in dirty, ripped uniforms. He also provided plenty of bats and equipment, another luxury in a time when many teams required players to supply their own bats.

Foster's Giants went on tour many times a year. They traveled by railroad in Pullman passenger cars. Passengers considered these well-furnished, comfortable coaches and sleeping cars the height of luxury. The American Giants went to Canada, out west to California in the winter, and south to Florida, where they played before tourists in large resort hotels. That the Giants traveled in such style and were able to draw large crowds was impressive to many blacks. It showed a level of class and professionalism that black teams had never achieved before. Foster soon became one of the most important owners in Negro baseball.

Andrew "Rube" Foster, owner and manager of the Chicago American Giants, poses with C. I. "Candy Jim" Taylor of the Indianapolis ABC's before the 1916 playoff series between the two teams. Also pictured are sports editors Elwood Knox (far left) and J. D. Howard of Indianapolis (second from right).

Even with such success, Foster believed that black players and owners would do better if they had an organized league. A league would allow them to set up schedules which would provide each team with organization and more financial security. It would make rules about players, trades, umpires, and other important details that establish a professional level of play. League play would also give fans a better way to compare black teams and provide for meaningful play-off games. With independent and barnstorming teams, it was often difficult to measure and appreciate the individual ball clubs. In all, an organized black league, Foster claimed, would give structure to black baseball where previously there was none.

In 1920 Foster formed the Negro National League. It included Foster's Chicago American Giants, the Cuban Stars (from Cincinnati), Dayton [Ohio] Marcos, Chicago Giants (another Foster team), Indianapolis ABC's, Kansas City Monarchs, Detroit Stars, and St. Louis Giants.

It was hard to keep the league together because the new teams had little money, yet Foster did it. Sometimes he had to pay hotel bills or train fares for teams that were stranded. Like a stern father, he made almost every decision in the new league. His decisions were good ones, and the Negro National League was able to survive and succeed.

In 1923, Foster helped with the formation of the Eastern Colored League. He felt two leagues would make Negro baseball even stronger. Six teams—the Brooklyn [New York] Royal Giants, Hilldale of Philadelphia, Lincoln Giants of New York, New Jersey's Bacharach Giants, Baltimore Black Sox, and the Eastern Cuban Stars—formed the league.

Because of his vision for black baseball, and because of his ability to lead and organize, Rube Foster is known as the father of the Negro leagues. He made the game better for everybody.

THE NEGRO LEAGUES

In November 1918, the bloody and destructive World War I ended. People looked forward to peace and good times. The era that followed was called the Jazz Age, after that lively, creative music. People had the leisure to dance, spend money, and go to the ballpark.

A year later, however, baseball experienced one of the worst scandals that can happen in any professional sport. In October 1919, the major league Chicago White Sox "threw" the World Series. In a deal with gamblers, a few of the top White Sox players lost games on purpose. The White Sox, by far the best team in baseball at the time, went on to lose the Series to a much weaker Cincinnati team. The gamblers had bet money on Cincinnati, and they won big. Some of their winnings went back to the dishonest White Sox.

The "fix" was discovered the next season and professional baseball was almost ruined. Fans would not support a crooked game. "We trust an outfielder or a shortstop," wrote the *Nation* magazine in 1920. "The man at bat is supposed to be doing his best." Eight players on the White Sox, which became known as the "Black Sox," were thrown out of baseball for life. People wondered if baseball would still be popular.

They did not wonder long, thanks to a player named George Herman "Babe" Ruth. Babe was an attraction: a smiling, round-faced man in a baggy New York Yankee uniform who could hit the ball a mile. "He was a parade all by himself," wrote newspaperman Jimmy Cannon.

Ruth started out as a lean, left-handed fastball pitcher for the Boston Red Sox, but he was such a good hitter that when he was traded to the New York Yankees—he was actually "sold" because the Red Sox owner needed the money—he became an outfielder. That way he could hit in every game. And nobody hit like Babe Ruth. Home runs, that is.

Ruth was helped by what became known as the "lively ball." In 1920 the major leagues began using a lighter, harder baseball. The old ball, called the "dead ball," was heavy and dense and very hard to hit over the fence. Even Ty Cobb and Honus Wagner seldom hit home runs. The top sluggers of the dead ball times hit only ten or twelve homers in a whole year, but Babe Ruth hit fifty-four home runs in 1920 alone! He would hit many more in the years to follow.

Babe Ruth and the home run changed baseball. Teams did not have to scratch and hustle for a single run if one man could step up to the plate and bash a homer. Fast runners and base-stealers were still important, but a chubby guy like Babe Ruth could win a game with one swing of the bat. The area in the right-field stands where many of his home runs landed was called "Ruthville." A sultan is a powerful ruler; a home run is sometimes called a swat—and Babe Ruth was called "the Sultan of Swat."

In 1920, black baseball also got livelier. Its popularity attracted many fine young athletes, and top-rate clubs formed all over the country. The best teams belonged to Rube Foster's new Negro National League. The league structure meant that fans would be able to watch top black teams compete against one another in a schedule of about sixty to seventy games.

The new Negro league had its share of problems, however. Many teams had trouble finding a home ballpark. Most black team owners did not have enough money to build their own parks. Baseball stadiums at that time were usually built by rich white businessmen who put their family name over the door. Only Foster's American Giants team had a home field, in Chicago. The others had to rent stadiums when the white professional teams were out of town. These arrangements were often difficult and made it hard to set up the Negro National League schedules.

Some teams, including the Chicago Giants and the Cuban Stars, were "road clubs," which meant they always traveled, playing league games in any stadium available. Without a "home," they never played in a stadium that they were used to or that gave them a "home field" advantage. Another problem with using other teams' stadiums was that often black players were not allowed to use the dressing rooms. They had to dress in their buses or in hotels, and drive to the park. After the game, when they were sweaty and dusty, they were unable to take a shower and clean up. The arrangement made many of them angry. They felt like second-class citizens.

But the keen competition of the Negro National League made the hardships worthwhile. Most of the players quit their regular jobs and only played baseball. It was a privilege, they said, to play, and it was a wonderful thing to get paid for it. Very few black people in America at that time could make a living in sports or entertainment. Those that did felt honored.

The Chicago American Giants were Negro League champions in 1921 with a record of 41–21. The Kansas City Monarchs came in second. There was no black World Series because there was not another league, but in 1923 the Eastern League was formed. At first Rube Foster, who had helped organize the new league, welcomed the new teams and the broader range of black baseball. But when Eastern clubs started signing players away from his Negro National League, Foster became enraged. Such stars as John Henry Lloyd, Oscar Charleston, and Biz Mackey—a fine catcher— went over to Eastern teams for more money. Foster responded by refusing to permit a World Series between the two leagues.

Negro league champions also took on white major league teams after the big-league season was over, as black teams had done many times through the years. In 1924, however, the commissioner of major league baseball, Judge Kenesaw Mountain Landis, put a stop to that. No big-league club could wear its own uniforms and play Negro league teams, Landis said. Nobody knows why Landis made this decision, but most people believed that Landis, who was always against the idea of allowing blacks to play in the major leagues, did not want white teams embarrassed by losing to black teams. From then on, white teams that played black squads were made up of players from different big-league clubs, and were known as "All-Stars."

By one count, black teams won seventy-four games and white big-league teams won forty-one when they played one another between 1920 and 1929. No official records were kept, so it is hard

Judge Kenesaw Mountain Landis, major league baseball's first commissioner, was a stern, unbending official. He is shown here in the 1930s.

to know the real numbers. But the results of known games show that the black players were just as good as the white major-leaguers. The record does not mean they were better. Many black players said that they played harder against whites because they had something to prove. The white players, on the other hand, might have looked at the games as exhibitions played for extra money. While they did not like to lose, they may have been more relaxed than usual. Nobody knows for sure. The only thing certain was that black players were still unable to play for major league teams, for major league salaries.

In 1924, Rube Foster allowed the first Negro League World Series. The promise of great games and enormous ticket sales was too good for him to pass up. The series featured the Kansas City Monarchs, winner of the National League, against the Hilldale club of Philadelphia in the Eastern League. There were ten games. They were tense, spectacular games, often decided by one run. Kansas City won the series five games to four. One game was tied when it was called due to darkness. Almost every year from then on Negro league baseball featured some kind of play-off or World Series.

League play in the 1920s gave much-needed organization to black baseball. When there is an official league, fans tend to pay more attention to it. When teams are independent and play opponents on all levels, it is hard to measure how good they are. The Negro National League changed that. Some people say it was the most important development in the history of black baseball.

Still, the new leagues and their money-poor teams struggled. Sometimes the games were rowdy and full of fights. The league did not have its own umpires. It was up to the home team to provide umpires, and many of these were incompetent. Bad umpiring allowed some games to get out of control. If the league did not punish unruly behavior, the players felt they could argue and curse umpires whenever they felt like it. Sometimes they even pushed and punched them.

When the fans saw this kind of behavior, they joined the players in "ragging" the ump, shouting and calling the umpire names. Sometimes fans came on the field to fight with the players or the umpires. The umpires were so worried about their safety that some began to carry guns with them on the field. An umpire in Georgia once pulled out a gun and actually fired it in the direction of the crowd.

Willie Wells, a fine player for the Newark Eagles, once got into a fierce argument with an umpire in St. Louis, only to drop his bat and run for the third-base-line seats. He jumped the fence and disappeared. Wells later explained that during the argument, he saw the ump reach into his back pocket. Certain that the umpire had a gun, Wells took off. The umpire proceeded to take out a whisk broom—not a pistol—and brush off home plate.

Rube Foster established strict rules for the league when he was in charge. He made sure players were disciplined when they caused trouble. Then, in 1926, at the age of forty-seven, Foster became very sick. He suffered a breakdown and was sent to a psychiatric hospital. His wife told doctors that Rube was imagining things and often acted strangely. He once insisted that the World Series was in progress and that he was needed to pitch. Foster never got well, and he died at age fifty-one.

Without Foster and his strong leadership, the Negro leagues' troubles increased. Money was always a problem. An owner who could not pay his team would disband it overnight, leaving the players with no money and nowhere to go. Teams were late for games or did not show up at all. Teams played in dirty uniforms. Stadiums were sometimes not clean or well maintained.

These problems went against the progress black baseball had made. They showed how hard it was to keep the leagues operating at a professional level. During the 1920s, however, black teams did get excellent publicity in black newspapers like the *Chicago Defender* and the *Pittsburgh Courier*. The *Courier*'s slogan was "Covering the Country Like a Tent," because black readers in all areas were able to buy it. The papers assigned sportswriters to cover the games and even to travel with the teams. Thousands of people read these papers, and they devoured news of their favorite players.

When players become stars, people want to know about them. Kids in black neighborhoods all over the country, particularly in the big cities of the North, wanted to be like Rube Foster or John Henry Lloyd. They wanted to wear the uniform of a Kansas City Monarch or a Bacharach Giant. They played more baseball, and they played it with a goal. Even though they could not hope to

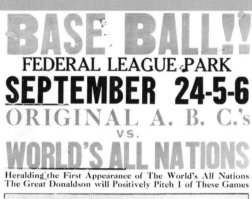

All nations, all colors. In 1916 Kansas City promoter J. L. Wilkinson toured this team of black, white, and foreign players around the country in a railroad car. Left-handed John Donaldson was one of the top pitchers in Negro baseball.

play on the green grass of Yankee Stadium next to Babe Ruth, they could dream of throwing as hard as Smokey Joe Williams in front of tens of thousands of fans in the Negro League World Series. That was something!

Although they did not have baseball cards or television sets, little black boys looked up to their new heroes. Napoleon Cummings was a small boy in Florida when he first saw John

Henry Lloyd play. Lloyd was a giant of a player, and he let Cummings carry his shoes and glove into the ballpark for him. Cummings, who later played for the Bacharach Giants, never forgot it.

Other black boys in small country towns may not have been so fortunate, but they, too, were touched by the black professional teams. They heard about these teams from their elders. Or they saw a black newspaper with stories about the players, and photographs. If they were lucky, they took a trip to a larger town to see a touring black squad.

Once in a while, black barnstorming teams came through small towns in their automobiles or buses. Sometimes they would stop for a drink of water or a bite at a restaurant. Sometimes they would go fishing. To small-town fans, many of the motorcars seemed flashy and the players looked well dressed. Some of them wore their team hats. Some showed the boys their gloves or their bats.

These boys were named James Bell, Leroy Paige, Josh Gibson, and Jimmie Crutchfield. They lived in places like Starkville, Mississippi; Mobile, Alabama; Buena Vista, Georgia; and Moberly, Missouri. They were to become a new generation of black ballplayers. If it had not been for the early black professional teams, none of these boys might have thought about life outside their own small towns. They would not have known baseball could be much more than a game played in weed-choked fields or on Sunday afternoon picnics. They would not have known baseball could be something with a future.

When the touring teams left in swirls of dust, these black, barefoot boys were never the same. They felt a magical sense of pride. They had seen their heroes. They had seen a vision of themselves.

THE CRAWS

The bus was a sleek, long-nosed, twenty-two-passenger Mack with a six-cylinder, seventy-nine-horsepower motor. It could cruise at sixty miles per hour and stop on a dime with its vacuum-booster brakes. It had cost $10,000. On its side, hand-painted in dark green letters, was PITTSBURGH CRAW-FORDS BASEBALL CLUB

The year was 1932, and the bus was just part of one of the classiest teams ever to play black baseball: This was Gus Greenlee's Pittsburgh Crawfords. On the road. Traveling in style.

At the wheel of the bus was Gus Greenlee himself, called Big Red because of his light skin and reddish hair. He was husky, with a jowly face. He often smoked a cigar. He was driving the bus because he owned it. He owned the entire ballclub—the uniforms and equipment, even the ballpark back in Pittsburgh. Gus Greenlee was a big man.

It was early March, and the bus was full of players headed for Hot Springs, Arkansas. One of the country's favorite resort areas, Hot Springs was named after the hot sulfur water that bubbled from the earth. The area's warm climate was perfect for spring training, and Greenlee had the money and the means to take his new ball club down there from cold Pittsburgh.

Most people called Greenlee a businessman. That was accurate, for he ran a big business in Pittsburgh. Other people, especially the police, called him a gangster, because Greenlee was a numbers king. Numbers, also known as Policy, was a form of illegal gambling, popular in poor communities.

Numbers was much like today's state lotteries: a large can held seventy-eight numbered chips or pebbles. Three were drawn out. Those three were the winning numbers. Players could put as little as a penny or a nickel on three numbers. The winner got back much, much more.

Numbers had to be played in secret. Men, even boys of ten or twelve, went around to houses and stores to collect numbers slips and bets. Everybody played a number: a birthday, an address, a license plate. Even dreams were interpreted into numbers. Playing the numbers was so popular that the men who ran the games grew very rich. Nobody paid taxes on the profits.

Gus Greenlee became one of the richest black men in Pittsburgh. His profits allowed him to buy the Crawford Grille, a popular black restaurant and meeting place on Wylie Avenue, which became a center for his business. Gamblers and entertainers went there. Athletes, politicians, and beautiful women lounged at the tables.

Even that was not enough for Big Red. Baseball was everybody's favorite game, and like many successful businessmen of

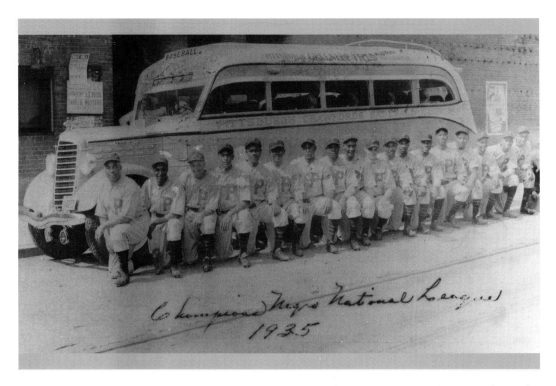

The 1936 Crawfords pose in front of Greenlee Field and the team's new Mack touring bus. This team, with five major league Hall of Famers in the lineup—Oscar Charleston, Satchel Paige, Josh Gibson, Judy Johnson, and Cool Papa Bell—was considered by many to be one of the finest squads ever assembled, regardless of color.

Kneeling (left to right): Oscar Charleston, Jimmie Crutchfield, Dick Seay, Sam Bankhead, Bill Harvey, Sam Streeter, Bill Perkins, Chester Williams, Theolic Smith, Harry Kincannon, Judy Johnson, Cool Papa Bell, Leroy Matlock, Ernest Carter, Josh Gibson, John Washington, Satchel Paige, unidentified rookie.

today, Greenlee wanted his own team. In 1931, he took over the Crawford Giants, a local Pittsburgh team that played in front of large crowds on the city's black North Side. He renamed the team Gus Greenlee's Pittsburgh Crawfords, and he was determined to turn it into a top professional black team. It would take money, but Greenlee had plenty of that. It would also mean getting better players than those on the Homestead Grays. The Grays, a team based in the steel-mill town of Homestead, just outside of Pittsburgh, had long been one of the best black ball clubs in the country.

In 1931, however, after the exciting decade of the 1920s, black baseball was in trouble. The Negro National League had folded after Rube Foster's death. The Eastern Colored League had collapsed two years earlier. Both were victims of something that affected both blacks and whites in the 1930s: the Great Depression.

After the stock market plunge of 1929, banks failed and many people lost all their savings. When businesses closed, people lost their jobs, and they could not find new ones. They formed long lines to get a meal at the soup kitchens that had been created to feed the hungry. Then, terrible droughts hit the Midwest, and many farmers lost everything. The government launched many programs to put people to work and to improve the economy, but very little worked. For an entire decade, Americans experienced hard, hard times.

Black workers, men and women, generally held unskilled jobs, and they soon experienced the hardest of these times. They were the first to be laid off. When unemployment was so high that white men were selling apples on street corners, blacks did not stand much chance of finding work. The jobs they could find paid twelve to fifteen dollars a week. Money was tight, and such luxuries as baseball games were the first to be cut out of a family's budget. It was no surprise that the ever-struggling Negro leagues would stumble and fall.

Bill Foster, the half brother of Rube Foster and a fine left-handed pitcher for many black teams, said that he lived on thirty-six cents a week in the Depression. "I always tell the boys about that rat I saw one day," Foster told author John Holway. "I saw a rat in the alley there sitting on a garbage can chewing on an onion. He was eating and just crying. That was all he could find, that onion. He was just eating and crying. . . . It just goes to show you—any time a rat's got to eat an onion, it's rough!"

In the midst of that kind of hardship, anybody with money to spend was king. Gus Greenlee had money, even if it was ill-gotten. With $100,000—a fortune in those days—he built Greenlee Field on Bedford Avenue. It would hold 6000 fans and would be the Crawfords' home field.

Greenlee Field meant more to black players and their fans than just a new ballpark. For years the Crawford Giants had played at Ammon Field, a local sandlot. Once in a while they played in Forbes Field, the home stadium of the big-league Pittsburgh Pirates.

Although the black teams enjoyed playing in Forbes Field, they had to pay a rental fee to do it. Also, black teams could not use the Forbes clubhouse. "After the game," said Ted Page, who played with the Crawfords and the Homestead Grays, "when we were hot and sweaty, we had to drive to the YMCA to take a shower. Here we had paid for the use of the stadium, but the club-house was locked."

By building his own park, Gus Greenlee was showing the community and the world that he would not use a white man's ballpark if he did not have to. Greenlee Field offered all its players first-class accommodations.

Greenlee then went about building his team. He decided to give the new young stars of black baseball offers they could not refuse. He offered Leroy "Satchel" Paige, a skinny, wisecracking

The meat of the Craws. Four members of the powerful 1932 Pittsburgh Crawfords get some advice from player/manager Oscar Charleston. From left: Charleston, Rap Dixon, Josh Gibson, Judy Johnson, Jud Wilson. "Those five!" said Cool Papa Bell. "I'd take those five guys over anybody!"

pitcher from the Cleveland Cubs, $250 a month. That was more than almost any other player in black baseball was making at the time.

Greenlee then approached some of the best of the Homestead Grays. He signed Oscar Charleston, the veteran outfielder and first baseman, to be his player-manager. He added third baseman Judy Johnson, and Ted Page, a fast outfielder. He signed Sam Streeter, a crafty left-handed pitcher. Then he signed the biggest new name in Pittsburgh, a slugging young catcher named Josh Gibson.

All this action enraged Cumberland "Cum" Posey, the owner and manager of the Grays. Posey had made the Grays one of the best teams in black baseball after the death of Rube Foster. He was a smart, determined, and educated man, and he wrote a baseball column in the *Pittsburgh Courier* to air his views. Even though he was glad to see Gus Greenlee bringing new money into black baseball, Posey was mad about losing his best players. Still, money was money, and Greenlee had more than Posey did. Aside from Paige, Crawford players were making salaries of $150–$200 a month. "That was *big* money," said Ted Page.

That spring, those Grays who had become Crawfords boarded Greenlee's nifty new bus to Hot Springs. They joined other new Crawfords, including Jimmie Crutchfield, the little outfielder; James Bell, nicknamed Cool Papa because he never got excited; and Ted "Double Duty" Radcliffe. Radcliffe was called Double Duty because he could pitch and catch in the same ballgame. Jud Wilson and Rap Dixon were two more of the hard hitters that Greenlee signed.

After a time in Hot Springs, the team began a tour of the South. They played small-town teams, semi-professional teams, and college teams. News of each game was sent back to the *Courier* and printed in it, so that Pittsburgh fans could follow the action.

Besides the game results, information about the conditions of poor black people living in the South was also reported. This news was interesting to the many blacks who had moved north from some of those same areas. Also, as it had earlier in the century, the *Courier*'s staff felt that it was important to publicize the hardships blacks continued to face in many parts of the country. Although some blacks had improved their lives by moving north, many Southern blacks still lived in shacks near railroads or cemeteries and made pennies a day as sharecroppers in the fields.

That news was offset by dispatches about the success of the mighty Crawfords. Satchel Paige threw nothing but scorching fastballs that reminded old-timers of the best of Smokey Joe Williams and Dick Redding. Josh Gibson was becoming such a walloper of home runs that the team advertised that he would hit two home runs every game. Of course he did not, but the fans loved the possibility.

From March 25 through July 21, the Crawford bus traveled all over the South. The team played 94 games in 109 days, with 13 games rained out. The bus logged 17,000 miles. In May, the team returned to Pittsburgh and Greenlee Field for a big series with the Grays. One game was to be played under new lights Greenlee had just had installed.

Each game was a battle, for even though the Crawfords had many stars, Cum Posey had enough veteran Grays to field a strong team. The Craws took three of five games, but it was not easy for them. They did show, however, that they were the new cream of Pittsburgh. In all, they beat the Grays in ten of nineteen games in 1932. "The Crawfords have taken the play away from the Grays," commented one Pittsburgh sportswriter.

Word of the Crawfords soon spread throughout the country. Everybody wanted to see them. Everybody looked for that sleek green bus. And the Crawfords obliged. The bus rolled up the miles. It was not uncommon for the Craws to travel all night— from Chicago to Philadelphia, for example—to arrive in time to play a doubleheader. The heat and exhaustion were hard on the players. Cool Papa Bell used to say that they had to learn how to sleep "lying down, sitting, or standing up."

When they did stop for lodging, they stayed in hotels, motor lodges, or the best inns they could find. Greenlee would not abide anything less. Still, they were black, and blacks were not readily served in many places in America. Once the Crawfords played a hard game in Ohio and had nowhere to shower until they

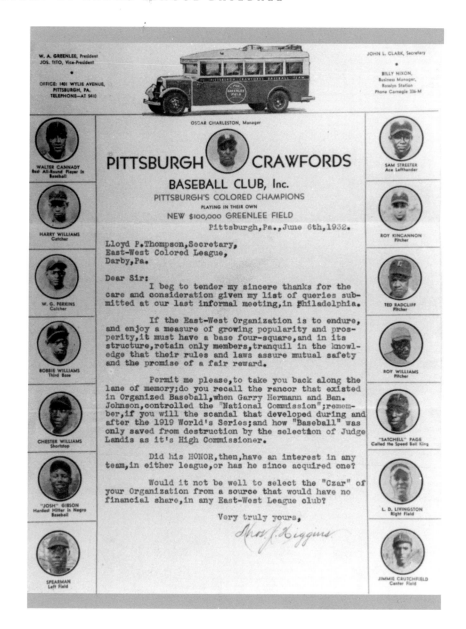

The Crawfords' flashy 1932 stationery even included a shot of the team's bus.
Owner Gus Greenlee spared no expense in promoting his new team.

convinced a lady who owned a rooming house to fill up a bathtub with hot water. Nine players cleaned up in that one tub of water.

Getting food was not much easier. One night, no restaurant between Akron and Youngstown, Ohio, would serve them, even though, as one player said, "Greenlee had his pocket bulging with money!" Sometimes they stopped at fruit stands and loaded up on cantaloupes, apples, and melons.

Usually the players packed bags of their own food—cold cuts, baloney sandwiches, cheese, pickles, chicken—and brought it on the bus. Keeping one's food wasn't always easy. A player would stow his sandwiches in the rack overhead and then drift off to sleep. The other players would swipe the sandwiches and pass them around. Everybody did it, but the victim was furious about it each time.

The Craws had a pitcher named Harry Kincannon. He was so light-skinned that many people felt he would not have been challenged had he tried to crack a major-league lineup as a white. His nickname was Tincan, and one night he came on the bus with several pieces of fried chicken. After he had eaten his fill, he stood up and showed the team a small pistol. He said, "Anybody eatin' my food tonight is gonna get it with this."

Then he put the pistol on his lap and fell asleep, and the pistol fell on the floor. One of his teammates took it and emptied the shells. Then the team passed around Tincan's chicken. After they ate the chicken, they collected the bones and tied them into a necklace, which they draped around the sleeping Kincannon's neck. When he awoke and discovered his bony necklace, the team howled with laughter. Kincannon was angry, but not angry enough to keep from laughing heartily himself.

The more the Crawfords traveled, the more famous they became. When they came into little towns, it was not uncommon for women to collect in hotel lobbies just to be near the players. Townsfolk often put on dances, sometimes outdoors under lights, and the team and crowds of people had a good time. When the game was on, the Crawfords were amazing to watch. With Paige pitching, Gibson, Dixon, and Wilson hitting long balls, and Bell and Crutchfield covering the outfield like a blanket, few teams—white or black—could take them.

In 1932, their first year, the Crawfords' record for the summer season was ninety-nine wins and thirty-six losses. There was no better team in Negro baseball, and yet the golden years of the Crawfords were just beginning. They were later to join a reorganized Negro National League and stand out as one of its best teams.

Most important, the Crawfords set a new standard as a sharp, professional black team in the face of the Great Depression, when hard times and lack of money destroyed many proud baseball teams. Each year the Craws posed for a photograph in front of their touring bus, which would be parked in front of Greenlee Field. There were Charleston, Paige, Gibson, Bell, Crutchfield, Johnson, and all the others. There was Tincan Kincannon.

And in the background was the money man, Gus Greenlee, "Big Red." Gus Greenlee's Pittsburgh Crawfords were big-time, and black fans everywhere knew it. The Craws were sensations!

BARNSTORMING AND "BEISBOL"

All ballplayers travel, but none traveled more than black baseball players. Their life was on the road, on the highway, on the train tracks, always heading for another town and another ballpark. They did not travel with guaranteed motel reservations, campers, or mobile homes. Often they had no place to stay at all. In many areas of the country, motels would not allow blacks to sleep in their beds. Sometimes they had no choice but to keep traveling and find "Negro" hotels. At other times, the players slept in the cars and buses. One team had tents that they pitched in fields.

Also, black touring teams were never sure they could use the rest rooms when they stopped at gas stations. Local police often harassed them, pulling them over for speeding or for not having the right license plates, or for other minor offenses. And often in Jim Crow America, black teams had no guarantee that they could stop and get something to eat. In those days there was no McDonald's at every stop. Restaurants often would not serve them.

Monte Irvin, an excellent infielder who later played in the major leagues, remembers when the Newark Eagles stopped at a diner in Alabama. As soon as they got off the bus, the woman owner shook her head: No, she would not serve them. When they asked to buy water, she allowed them to use the well out back. There was a gourd fashioned as a water scoop and the players drank from it. When they were done, they saw the woman take the gourd and break it into little pieces. It would never be used again. "How could she hate us so?" asked Irvin.

Sometimes the teams stayed with local black residents. Ted Page of the Grays and Crawfords remembered, "There would be two or three of us in one bed. Two players in one house. We were scattered in private homes all over. That was all we could afford." And Page remembered that when the players did stay in hotels, the conditions could be pretty bad. "There was a rooming house in Arkansas," Page said, "that when you turned on the lights you'd see the bedbugs run for cover. There were hotels where you'd sleep with the lights on, because bugs would come out with lights off and keep you up all night."

The teams had no choice. They had to travel and had to put up with the hardships. Even when the best of the Negro leagues were in operation, league games took only a part of team schedules. During the rest of the year the teams traveled the circuit, touring, barnstorming, finding a game. The reason was simple: a paycheck. To get one, a team would hop in a school bus or in a pair of cars, throw the equipment in a box tied to the trunk, stock bedrolls and some personal effects, and take off.

Today the closest thing to the touring spectacle of black teams is Eddie Feigner's King and His Court (a traveling four-man soft-ball team) and the Harlem Globetrotters. The Globetrotters, in fact, were founded by Abe Saperstein, a Chicago promoter who also booked many games for black baseball teams. The black Globetrotters always play the white Washington Generals, a team that travels with them and goes through set routines on the court. Before each game the Globetrotters stand in a circle and put on a tricky passing exhibition to the tune of "Sweet Georgia Brown." During the game the Trotters mix clowning with superb drib-bling, passing, and shooting. They joke with the fans and play tricks on the Generals and the referees.

Modern-day audiences may not know that the Globetrotters' routines were first perfected by barnstorming baseball teams, although the black teams could not afford to bring along their own foe. Instead, they played any team they could find. America was crazy about baseball in the first part of the twentieth century, and most towns had a team. Often a town would put together an all-star team to play the black squads. The growing fame of some of the good Negro teams and of the big stars made their arrival the event of the year.

"The Grays traveled all season long," said Judy Johnson, the star third baseman. "Every day you were going, you'd go and ride over those hills. Every two hours you had to average a hundred miles. With nine men in the car! That's what we averaged." And, according to Johnson, not all the police were unfriendly: "The cops all knew us; we had 'Homestead Grays' on the sides and they'd call, 'Hey, Homestead Grays!' and we'd be going like a bat out of hell."

When a black team came to town, it knew it had to put on a show. Usually that meant playing great baseball, which is what the team did best, but sometimes it meant some pregame entertainment. During warm-up exercises called pepper games, the players tossed the ball through their legs, behind their backs, down their arms, and off their feet. Players could handle a baseball blindfolded, and some of them did just that as a warm-up gimmick. They could play tricks with the ball, make it appear and disappear, spin it, toss it, and catch it in any way and at any angle. Sometimes they played "phantom" pepper, where they did every move, every motion, without a ball. The fans were amazed by it; the fans loved it.

Other times black players showcased their talents. Satchel Paige and other great pitchers would see how many pitches they could throw over a gum wrapper. Some players would put on sprinting demonstrations. Sometimes they would simply stand close to the fans. Many players remember visiting small farm towns where children had never seen blacks before. The kids touched the players' skin and ran their fingers through their hair.

The biggest attraction, of course, came when black teams squared off against major leaguers. Back in the twenties and thirties, major league stars, such as Grover Cleveland Alexander and the Cardinals' Dizzy Dean, would play off-season games with semiprofessional teams. Generally the competition was healthy. Sometimes black teams had scores to settle. Many big-leaguers felt about blacks as had Cap Anson, the early black-hating star. Such players as Al Simmons and the great Ty Cobb never made a secret of their dislike of black players. Their feelings only brought out the fierce competitiveness of Negro-leaguers.

Frank Demaree, a member of the Chicago Cubs, once remarked publicly that he did not think much of a Satchel Paige team. When Paige pitched in an exhibition game against Demaree, he intentionally walked the bases loaded before Demaree came to the

"Seven steps and a slide" was what James "Cool Papa" Bell said he needed to get from first to second base. Here he slides into third base for the Homestead Grays in the 1930s. "People told me I was faster than anyone," Bell always said.

plate. Then, as Demaree stood at the plate and waited, Paige called his outfielders to the dugout. He told his infielders to sit down. And he proceeded to strike Demaree out with three pitches.

It would be wrong, however, to suggest that most white major leaguers were prejudiced. Many stars, such as Dizzy Dean and Jimmy Foxx of the Philadelphia Athletics, relished their play against black teams and had nothing but praise for them. Black teams had few problems with their white opponents, no matter what the level of play. Sometimes the fans could be nasty, though, calling black players the same insulting names that blacks had heard through the years. Cool Papa Bell remembered when some fans threw urine from "bedpots" at the players. But usually good baseball fans appreciated good baseball, and they knew the black teams could deliver it.

During the Depression, however, it was often difficult to draw good crowds with baseball alone. Many teams tried to spice up the show. They signed celebrity athletes, such as Olympic sprinting hero Jesse Owens, to appear with them. Babe Didrickson, a white female Olympic track star and a celebrated golfer, once pitched for a black touring team. She would throw only for a couple of innings, but it was enough to show her stuff. She had a good curve-ball and could get many batters out.

Another big attraction were the House of David teams from Michigan. Members of a religious settlement, the men of the House of David let their hair and beards grow very long. They were excellent players. Black players called them "Whiskers" and drew big crowds whenever they competed against them. The House of David players also liked to put on pepper and "phantom" ball demonstrations before the game. One House of David player, a pitcher named Ben Benson, actually made it to the major leagues for a brief stay.

In 1929, Jack Marshall, a fine black player, put together two touring teams for a Canadian promoter who mixed the games with a band and a minstrel show. The group traveled through Canada in four trucks and slept in a big tent. The promoter offered a reward of $500 to any local team that could beat his black squads. "We never lost a game under those conditions," Marshall said.

After the game the promoter opened a midway with the minstrel show, and after that, the band played for dancing. It was a remarkable traveling road show, and it drew people from hundreds of miles around. It played only in Canada, however, for the promoter could not get the necessary licenses and permits in the United States.

Perhaps the best new barnstorming attraction appeared in 1930, when the Kansas City Monarchs put together a system of

"The Whiskers." The white House of David team from Benton Harbor, Michigan, was a popular touring team that often matched up with black barnstorming squads. They are shown here in the 1930s.

portable lights. It was the first such system in Negro baseball, and it consisted of generators on trucks and light poles that were erected around the edge of the field. To help batters see the ball, a big canvas was put up in center field to create a better background.

Because the poles were not very tall and the lighting not very bright, playing conditions were not the best. When the ball went above the lights, nobody could see it. Pitchers with jumpy curve-balls and quick fastballs were almost impossible to hit. That year, in an extra-inning game under the lights, Smokey Joe Williams, the famous fastball pitcher for the Homestead Grays, struck out twenty-seven batters and beat the Monarchs, 1–0. It was hard enough to see Smokey Joe's pitches in the light of day, much less in

Light up the sky! Night baseball came to America in 1930 with the Kansas City Monarchs and their portable lighting system. With poles and generators on trucks, the lights were up and shining in a few hours. Fans loved to see the touring Monarchs play under the stars.

bad night light. The lighted games were big attractions, however, and many fans who worked all day flocked to see the teams in the cooler night air.

Another way to attract customers was clowning. Black players loved the game and they easily developed high jinks on the field. It was fun for them to add the routines to the regular games. Often clowning meant nothing more than adding an extra hop or a fancy backhand flip during a play. Sometimes it meant joking out loud between a pitcher and a batter. Once, when Josh Gibson hit a long home run off Satchel Paige, he yelled out to the mound as he was rounding the bases, "If you could cook, Satch, I'd marry ya!" Sometimes players would do vaudeville routines, such as carrying a newspaper into the field. The player would cut a hole in it to see the action and throw down the paper just in time to make a catch, or he would pretend to keep reading while another fielder had to retrieve the ball.

Sometimes whole teams were devoted to clowning, and were named Clowns. Teams from Miami, Cincinnati, and Indianapolis called themselves the Clowns. There were also teams called the Tennessee Rats, the Zulu Cannibals, and the Ethiopian Clowns. The players painted their faces, took on African names like Selassie, and even wore wigs and grass skirts. They performed war dances with savage cries and spears, all to the delight of their audiences.

With other teams, clowning often involved just a few players who had developed routines similar to those of vaudeville. Sometimes players would run to third instead of first after a hit. Some wore top hats or oversize gloves. Goose Tatum, who later starred with the Harlem Globetrotters, was a fine first baseman and also one of the funniest showmen. He wore an oversize glove on his foot, and he made crazy faces and outrageous remarks.

Pepper Bassett, a catcher for many top teams, sat in a rocking chair behind the plate when he played with the Crawfords and the Cincinnati Clowns. Bassett had a great arm. "He can knock a gnat off a dwarf's ear at 100 yards," owner Gus Greenlee said of Bassett. "It was easy catching in the chair," said Bassett himself. "And they went for it." Of course, good clowning players often made extra money with their acts.

But, then as now, there were mixed feelings about clowning. Many players and sportswriters said clowning brought out the worst stereotypes that whites held about blacks. Some were insulted by it, claiming it brought back the days of minstrel shows in which blacks were depicted as smiley, lazy, and foolish characters who spoke bad English with heavy Southern accents. Other players felt people would get the idea that clowning was all black teams could do.

Cool Papa Bell, for example, remembers when a House of David team played donkey baseball. Usually when black teams encountered House of David squads, they played conventional games which the fans enjoyed. In this game, Bell said, players on both teams had to ride donkeys instead of running to the bases. For Bell and some of the others, this was carrying things too far. "I told the manager I didn't sign a contract to ride a donkey, and I didn't," Bell said.

Many players called the clowning "monkeyshines," a term that is still used for "shenanigans." Nat Strong and other Negro league promoters hated clowning, and often refused to book games between clowns and league teams.

Wendell Davis, a sportswriter for the *Pittsburgh Courier*, wrote angry editorials about clowning. "Negroes must realize the danger in insisting that ballplayers paint their faces and go through minstrel show revues before each ballgame. Every Negro in public life stands for something more than the role he is playing. Every Negro in the theatrical and sports world is somewhat of an ambassador for the Negro race—whether he likes it or not."

Though clowning was not a big part of Negro baseball, it did show the fun and ease with which the black teams played the game. And in hard times it brought out customers. Fans black and white loved the antics, and the players often did, too. But clowning never overshadowed the real attraction of the black teams: their serious, solid baseball, and their remarkable performers.

Players such as Josh Gibson, Cool Papa Bell, and Buck Leonard were a pleasure to watch. So was Satchel Paige. As his fame grew— fame based on his ability and on his showmanship—people everywhere wanted to see him play. Paige himself said, "We played everywhere, in every ballpark. And we won, won like we invented the game."

After the summer league ended, and after a brief fall and early winter season in California, Florida, and Texas, many black players went south to Cuba, Mexico, Puerto Rico, and Venezuela. The game there, called *beisbol*, was hotter than the weather. The fans were wild—they were called *franticos*, "frantic ones"—and great players were heroes. Many white major- and minor-league players traveled there to work out problems or hone skills, or to get back into shape after an injury. For the white players, playing south was the mark of a hard worker. For blacks, however, it was money. They knew no such thing as a vacation or an off-season. Many black players played year-round for their entire careers.

The most important thing about winter *beisbol* was the absence of a color line. Whites played with blacks, Puerto Ricans,

Beisbol was what the Latins called it, and black players like Bill Byrd, Josh Gibson, and Dick Seay (left to right), shown here in their Santurce, Puerto Rico, uniforms, loved to play winter ball in countries south of the border. In front is a lucky batboy.

Mexicans, and Cubans in front of Latin crowds. Good baseball was only one result. Another was that it showed the color bar to be ridiculous. Players of all colors could play together and compete against one another.

The more honest of the major league owners realized this. Many watched players like Paige, Bell, and Gibson, and saw how valuable they would be if they were white. Earl Mack of the Philadelphia Phillies told Cool Papa Bell, "I could afford to pay a hundred thousand dollars for you." The other top black players heard the same thing. In the meantime, owners of Latin teams did pay the black Americans well. Many American owners of Negro league teams considered the Latin owners to be their biggest competition for their top players. At one point they hired lawyers to sue players who left their teams to play south of the border. Yet that did not keep such players as the Newark Eagles' Willie Wells from staying in Mexico even after the summer season began.

Said Wells, "Not only do I get more money playing here, but I live like a king. . . . I've found freedom and democracy here, something I never found in the United States. I was branded a Negro in the States and had to act accordingly. Everything I did, including playing ball, was regulated by my color. Well, here in Mexico I am a man. I can go as far in baseball as I am capable of going."

Black players liked to play in Latin countries because they were treated well both on and off the field. They were free to go anywhere, eat anywhere, do anything. The housing was not usually fancy. Luxury hotels were built for tourists and generally not available to visiting players, but, overall, conditions were better than those in the United States, especially along American back roads.

Also, foreign baseball did not demand as much traveling. The players had more time to relax, eat ice cream, or play card games such as pinochle. Many players found that speaking Spanish was not difficult for them. "When you get hungry enough," Josh Gibson once told his sister, "you find yourself speaking Spanish very well."

There were problems. When the water was bad, players might get very sick. The heat was often unbearable. Players found themselves exhausted after just a few innings. Bus rides between cities could be treacherous. Winding, two-lane roads cut through the mountains, and players wondered if team buses might topple down the steep cliffs.

Cuba was a favorite spot of visiting black players. The island is close to the United States, and Cubans were enthusiastic fans. There were also many great Cuban players. One was Luis Tiant, a crafty pitcher, whose son Luis Jr. later became a fine major-league

Quincy Troupe (left), a top Negro catcher, and Ray Dandridge, an all-star third baseman, played for the Mexican Marianao team.

pitcher. Cuban ball was wild and rough. American black players got into more fights with Cubans than anybody else. Often the fans ran onto the field. Police officers stood at the corners of the stands to keep order.

It was in the Dominican Republic that black ballplayers had their scariest experience. In 1937, agents from that island country came to the United States to recruit the best black players. The country's dictator, Rafael Trujillo, had a baseball team, but it was in last place in the Dominican Republic league. In Latin American countries, a politician needed a good team to remain popular. Trujillo had taken over the government by armed force, and now he figured he had to rule the country's baseball competition.

Trujillo's men offered big money—about $3000—to Satchel Paige, and then Paige put out the call to other top players. The offers varied from $1000 to $2500 for six weeks of play, with all

Cool Papa Bell (right) and Josh Gibson, playing for the Rafael Trujillo team in the Dominican Republic in 1937. Their smiles vanished when they were told that they had to win or they might not leave the country alive. They won.

expenses paid. Paige persuaded Cool Papa Bell, Leroy Matlock, Sammy Bankhead, and Harry Williams, all members of the Pittsburgh Crawfords, to "jump" their American contracts and make the trip. Gus Greenlee was furious, but the hard times had hit even his pocketbook, and he could not come close to matching the money his players were to get from Trujillo.

In Santo Domingo, the capital of the country, Paige and the other Crawfords were joined by Josh Gibson. Trujillo's team now had some of the best talent in baseball. According to Paige and

Bell, Trujillo's men told the team that they had to win "or else." "Or else" meant that they would be put to death by a firing squad. To make sure the American players knew Trujillo meant business, they were kept in their hotel when they weren't playing and were guarded around the clock.

The games were popular events, attended by many politicians and government officials. Also in the crowd were Trujillo's uniformed soldiers. They carried rifles with bayonets, and the blades glittered in the sunlight. The American players said they could not miss seeing those long bayonets. Nevertheless, they played, and played well, and the Trujillo team went from last place to first. The players were later told that if they had not won, Trujillo might have been overthrown and the players would not have gotten out of the country alive.

As it was, they stayed six weeks, collected their fat paychecks, and quickly got on a boat for home. None of them ever returned. They did take their uniforms back with them, though, and with a few extra players, they toured the Midwest as the Trujillo All-Stars.

Negro league owners, including Gus Greenlee and Cum Posey, were furious with the jumpers. They vowed to bar them from playing in the Negro leagues. "These men must realize that the league is far larger and more powerful than they are," said Greenlee.

But that was not really true. The players who went to the Dominican Republic were some of the best, and teams were eager to re-sign them. The players themselves, remembering the soldiers and the bayonets, were happy to stay far away from that frightening country.

SATCHEL

When he was a boy of ten he could throw a stone and hit a bird in a tree. When he was sixty-two he got out of a rocking chair and struck out major league hitters. For his entire life, Satchel Paige was *something*.

Without question, Paige was black baseball's brightest star. He was an ace pitcher, a traveling road show. He was the greatest all-time attraction in the Negro leagues, and an irresistible favorite among white fans. Anybody who knew baseball knew the name Satchel.

Tall and skinny as a cane pole, Paige stood on the mound and wiggled his glove or tugged on the bill of his cap. He wound up twice, twirled his arm like a windmill, and threw pellets across the plate. Nobody ever blazed a baseball faster or threw it with more control. And then Satchel smiled, or jabbered, or made a crack so wise that players and fans alike shook their heads in amazement.

"When Satchel would show up," said teammate Jimmie Crutchfield, "it was like the sun coming out from behind the clouds."

Paige shone so magnificently because he was so good and so full of fun, and he never seemed to grow old. He titled his autobiography *Maybe I'll Pitch Forever* and, although he did not pitch forever, he played for several decades. He crossed baseball's color line as did no other man.

Paige was a star of the great Negro league teams of the 1930s, such as the Pittsburgh Crawfords and the Kansas City Monarchs. Then he starred for the Cleveland Indians, the major league team that won the 1948 World Championship. He even pitched three scoreless innings for the Oakland A's in 1965, when he was almost sixty years old. No other Negro league performer—not Josh Gibson nor Buck Leonard nor Cool Papa Bell—was able to span time like that. To do what Paige did, Babe Ruth, who died in 1948, would have had to have played alongside Lou Gehrig in the 1920s—which Ruth did—*and* with Mickey Mantle in the 1950s.

Satchel's real name was Leroy. He was born in 1906—although he told people he never knew the year of his birth—in Mobile, a middle-sized waterfront city in southwestern Alabama. He was one of thirteen children in a very poor family. His father was a gardener, and his mother washed clothes for white families.

As a small boy, Leroy worked odd jobs to earn pennies for his family. One of these was toting suitcases at the train station. He could earn a nickel for each bag, or satchel, that he carried. Later, he liked to tell people how he put a stout pole on his shoulders in order to heft more bags. Once, he was carrying so many bags that one of the other redcaps said, "You look like a walking satchel tree!" That name stuck. For the rest of his life Leroy was called

Satchel, or just Satch, or sometimes Satchelfoots because the shoes on his size-12 feet looked to some people like walking suitcases. It was a name like no other for a player like no other.

At age ten, Satchel started playing baseball for his school team. His strong arm soon made him a star player. He played better than he attended classes, though. Satchel was not a good student nor was he interested in school. Outside class, he got in fights and other trouble. When he was twelve he was caught stealing from a toy store. It was decided that he would be sent to a special school for problem boys in Mt. Meigs, Alabama.

At the Mt. Meigs school he stayed out of trouble and worked on pitching a baseball. As an adult, he said that the four years he spent there probably prevented him from going into a life of crime. In 1923 he left Mt. Meigs. He was seventeen, weighed about 140 pounds, and was six feet four inches tall. His long, lean arms hung loosely when he walked. He needed a job badly, and the job he did best was throw a baseball.

Satchel's brother Wilson played for the Mobile Tigers, a black semi-pro team. When Satchel showed the team's manager what he could do, the manager signed him up immediately. His pay was only one dollar a game, but that was a gold mine to him. He was to play baseball for a living for the next forty years.

Paige played for several teams around Mobile in those early years. In 1926 he went to the Chattanooga [Tennessee] Black Lookouts in the Negro Southern League. Stories differ about just how good Paige was back then, but nobody argues about how hard he could throw the ball. Kicking his long leg in the air and reaching back with his long right arm, Paige threw the ball with the snap of a bullwhip. He threw nothing but fastballs. He had blinding speed, even if he did not always find the plate.

"When I first broke in I had to pitch batting practice for Chattanooga," he said. "They had five or six good pitchers, and I couldn't get the ball across the plate the way they wanted me to."

Gaining control of his pitches did not take long, though, and Paige was soon winning almost every game he pitched. He would strike out as many as eighteen batters a game. In 1928 he joined the Birmingham [Alabama] Black Barons of the Negro National League. Birmingham was the best team in the South, and one of Negro baseball's top pro squads. His salary was $275 a month— more than the buck a game he first made in Mobile. Paige's reputation soon spread all over the South. Everybody was talking about him. Everybody wanted to see him. As many as eight thousand fans showed up when he pitched for the Black Barons. "That was something in Birmingham," said Jimmie Crutchfield.

As Paige developed as a pitcher, he also became a showman. He had different names for his pitches. He called his fastball a "bee ball" because it hummed. Or he called it his "jump ball" or his "trouble ball." Sometimes he just called it "Long Tom," as if it had a personality of its own.

He also made a habit of walking very slowly to the mound. He would look like he was tired and sleepy. He had a long face and droopy eyes, and he looked like a sad sack. But then he started throwing, and there was nothing sleepy about his pitches.

Because he was so popular, Paige was constantly offered extra money to play for other teams. He usually did it. Sometimes he jumped from his team for a few days, or a month, or for the rest of the season. It was a practice that made Paige many enemies. Team owners said he was undependable. Some fellow players did not like that he could just pack up and go anywhere he wanted, while they had to stay and fulfill their contracts. Yet when Paige showed up

Satchel Paige of the Cleveland Indians. After twenty-six years of Negro league ball, Paige joined the major league Indians in July 1948, at age forty-two. His record that year was 6–1.

and threw Long Tom, few could resist his performance or his personality.

In 1932 Paige was the best black player anywhere, and every owner wanted him. The man with the fattest bankroll was Gus Greenlee in Pittsburgh, and he signed Paige to play for his Crawfords. It was the beginning of the golden years of the

Crawfords as they stormed through the country in their new bus. Naturally, Paige was promoted wherever the Craws went.

SATCHEL PAIGE, said one of the team's banners, GUARANTEED TO STRIKE OUT THE FIRST NINE MEN!

Of course, Paige could not always perform such a feat, but often he did. That year the Crawfords won ninety-nine games and lost thirty-six. Satchel won twenty-three and lost only seven.

Chester Washington wrote in the *Pittsburgh Courier,* "If 30,000 attend, 29,999 will be hoping to see the slow-moving fastball-pitching Satchel Paige. Satch is one of the best natural showmen in baseball. He is to Negro baseball today what Babe Ruth and Carl Hubbell were to the majors in yesteryears."

While Paige stayed with the Crawfords for the next few years, he still jumped to play for teams who dangled ready money in front of him. Many times Gus Greenlee himself set up these deals. Often he did not, and then jumping got Paige in trouble. But it did make him money. He was easily the highest-paid player in Negro baseball, earning as much as $30,000–$40,000 a year during the Depression. The average yearly pay of Paige's team-mates was much less, about $4000.

Paige was never one to save his cash. He loved cars—usually red Lincoln convertibles—and clothes. He dressed in flashy suits and two-toned shoes. He loved good times and staying out late— what newspaper reporters called "carousing." He loved to strum a ukulele (a tiny guitar) and sing twangy songs. He drove fast and often got speeding tickets. Ted "Double Duty" Radcliffe, Paige's teammate on the Crawfords, once told a story about how a judge in Kansas fined Paige $40 for speeding. When the judge asked him if he had anything to say, Paige took out $80. "Here you go, Judge," he said, "'cause I'm comin' back through tomorrow."

For the rest of the 1930s, Paige dominated black baseball. He played all over: in the Negro leagues with the Crawfords, in Mexico, even with a white semi-pro team in North Dakota. And he barnstormed on his own. He pitched seriously, or he showed his tricks. He loved to take infield practice when the team was doing fancy tosses. He could flip the ball to first base—behind his back or through his legs. In small towns he would put nails in a board and then pound them into the wood with fastballs thrown from sixty feet away.

In 1934 he put together the Satchel Paige All-Stars and played a series of games in California against the Dizzy Dean Major League All-Stars. Dean was a joking, popular pitcher for the St. Louis Cardinals, and he was almost as outrageous a figure as Paige. Because Paige loved playing against Dean, and Dean admired Paige, the two of them put on great displays. "The best pitcher I ever seen is ol' Satchel Paige," Dean often said. "My fastball looks like a change of pace alongside that li'l pistol bullet Satch shoots up to the plate."

One game, in Hollywood Park, had no score for thirteen innings. Paige and Dean both pitched brilliantly. In a late inning, Dean himself got a double off Paige. Paige called time, went over to Dean on second base, and said, "Dizzy, I don't have no runs and it look like you tryin' to get one. And it can't be like that." Then he struck out the side. Paige's All-Stars finally won the game, 1–0.

Everywhere he went, Paige talked. "I was born with control. I take two awful hot baths a day. I keep moving all the time on the diamond and I eat nothing but fried foods," he said.

He even invented new pitches. He called one pitch his "eephus" pitch, because it put batters to sleep like ether. He dipped his arm low and threw a submarine pitch.

Perhaps his most amazing pitch was the "hesitation" pitch. He would wind up, just as if he were going to pour a fastball down the plate, and then he would stop, or hesitate, in mid-motion. With his front foot on the ground and body still for an instant, his arm would come through with a hot fastball. Paige told his teammates that he developed the pitch as a boy, when he got in rock-throwing fights. When a boy hid behind a tree, he would stick his head out, then duck when Satchel threw. So Satchel would pretend to throw the rock, the kid would duck, and then Satch would really throw—and hit him. It got Satch into trouble, but it also developed that remarkable pitch.

The hesitation pitch threw batters off and was so effective and tricky that it was later ruled illegal. Today it would be called a balk.

In 1937, after Paige made his famous jump to the Dominican Republic and Rafael Trujillo, he was once again in trouble with Negro league owners. They vowed to keep him from ever pitching in their leagues again. He was "banned for life."

To Paige, the ban only meant that he would move on. He went down to Mexico and pitched almost every day. But in Mexico during 1938 Paige nearly lost everything. Toward the end of the summer season, his arm got sore. He was thirty-two and had pitched for many years, but this was the first time he had ever had arm trouble. He also was sick from the food in Mexico. He said he had "the miseries." Finally his arm hurt so much he could not lift it above his head, much less throw a baseball. He went back to the United States, where doctors told him he might not ever pitch again.

Not even Satchel Paige could get work without an arm, and he was worried that his career was over. It was J. L. "Ralph"

Wilkinson, owner of the Kansas City Monarchs, who hired him to travel with a second team Wilkinson had formed. Once again called Satchel Paige's All-Stars, the squad traveled around, advertising Paige's appearance. All he could do, however, was throw a few weak pitches or play first base. Satchel Paige was beginning to look like a has-been.

Then it came back. His arm recovered in 1939, and he began to throw hard without any pain. No one could explain it, but it was back. Long Tom, the trouble ball, and the hesitation pitch came with it. For the next ten years, Paige stayed with the Monarchs— the top team, of course—and helped them become the champions of Negro baseball. Once again he toured all over, a tour made even more successful because of the Monarchs' system of portable lights. "Mr. Wilkinson and me invented night baseball," Paige liked to say.

Drastic changes came to baseball in the 1940s, and Paige was affected by them. Beginning in 1942, many major league players were called away from their teams to serve in World War II. But professional baseball was still played, even though less talented players filled in. Teams had players who had been classified "4-F"—unfit to be soldiers because of a physical condition or injury.

The St. Louis Browns even played a one-armed outfielder named Pete Gray. He was able to field the ball with his gloved hand and, in a single motion, flip the glove off and throw the ball. His ability, however, did not impress black players. "The only thing a one-armed white man can do as good as a two-armed black man," grumbled black pitching star Chet Brewer, "is scratch the side that itches."

Many people thought the war years would be the time that major league teams would finally sign blacks, and several owners wanted to do it. Rumors spread in every big-league city where a team needed talent. Satchel Paige's name always came up.

By then, there was no doubt in anybody's mind that black players were good enough to perform in the majors. For twenty years black teams with players like Paige had beaten white big-leaguers. Paige's black all-stars had pounded Dizzy Dean and his All-Stars in head-to-head competition. Later Paige outpitched Bob Feller, the great Cleveland Indian fastball pitcher.

One encounter in particular shows how good Paige was and how much respect big-leaguers had for him. While he was playing in California in the winter of 1935, Paige was asked to pitch batting practice to young Joe DiMaggio. DiMaggio would go on to become a great New York Yankees star and one of the greatest players of all time, but then he was still a green, minor-league outfielder.

"Joe told me to bear down. Pitch just like we was playin' a game," Paige said later. "The first three he didn't even see. I was throwin' pretty fair. Ninety miles an hour easy. He come out and talk to me and he said, 'You really throwin' that ball or are you shootin' it?' I said, 'I'm throwin' it. I got a little hop on it.' He said, 'You ever hit anybody?' I said, 'No.' He said, 'If you do, you gonna kill somebody.'"

A few days later Paige pitched against DiMaggio in an all-star game. "Joe played against me. He come up and I struck him out twice," Paige said. "Next time he hit a long one foul down the first base line before I struck him out again. Next time he come up I threw him a curveball and he doubled. That's when he said he was ready for the big leagues."

But was Paige ready for the big leagues? When World War II ended in 1945, he still was not there. No black player was. Paige was almost forty, an age when most pitchers have long since quit. His arm, however, was twice as old. Paige had pitched year-round for twenty years. There is no official count, but he estimated he had appeared in two thousand games. One year alone, he claimed, he pitched in 153 games. He'd played for hundreds of teams in almost every state and in several foreign countries.

And yet he was still throwing. He did not have the enormous speed any longer, but he had his pinpoint control. He could put the ball anywhere he wanted it. He perfected a wicked curve, and he spiced things up with crazy motions, double wind-ups, windmills, and tricky pitches that threw batters off-stride. He could still get people out. People could not believe it, and they continued to travel for miles to see the great Satchel Paige. He traveled thousands of miles to give them that chance.

Paige himself was amazed.

"People say, 'Satchel, people are all around you lookin' at you,'" he said. "'A fella back there just want to put his hands on ya.' I say, 'Lotta people don't think I'm human I been playin' so long and pitchin' everyday.' So yeah, they want to put their hands on me."

In 1945 he was still playing for the Kansas City Monarchs. He had done just about everything a man could do in baseball. Except one thing: he had never worn a major league uniform. And Paige, who never worried or wondered about much, started to worry and wonder if that would ever happen. On his Monarchs team that year was a rookie infielder named Jackie Robinson. He was a good player. Paige told everybody that. But Jackie Robinson was to be much more. He would be something that would finally allow the great Satchel Paige to achieve the last remaining goal in his remarkable baseball career.

THE EAST-WEST ALL-STAR GAMES

Even though baseball is a team game, the individual player shines. One player bats. One player pitches. One player fields the ball. Individual acts combine to make up a chain of events in which the ball is thrown, hit, and (maybe) caught. Runners motor around the bases. Umpires get in position. Fans jump to their feet and cheer. A single player can hit a home run and account for a score entirely on his own. Or he can be one part of many moves—a single, a bunt, a walk, a stolen base, a sacrifice—to produce a run. Fans root for their favorite team at the same time that they follow their favorite player. Individuals can stand out. A single pitcher can dominate a whole game, or one batter can produce all of a team's score.

That is why baseball fans love all-star games. In them they can see individual stars come together on remarkable "dream" teams. They can see a game played all-out—unlike football or basketball

all-star games, where the fear of injury often makes the action very casual. They can see players matched up against those in opposite leagues, something that otherwise happens only during the World Series, because the American and National Leagues do not have inter-league play. All other professional sports do.

All-star games are old and popular events. The first major league all-star game was played on July 6, 1933, in Chicago's Comiskey Park. It was the idea of Arch Ward, a sports editor of the *Chicago Tribune*. Chicago was hosting the 1933 World's Fair, called The Century of Progress. This exposition was an attempt to stimulate the Depression-era economy by encouraging people to travel and spend money. Remarkable exhibits of business and technology, many with an eye to what life would be like in the future, drew millions of people to the city.

Arch Ward thought it would be a great attraction if major league players came together in Chicago for what he called a "dream game." He thought it would be a one-time event to coincide with the World's Fair. The officials of big league baseball liked the idea. Attendance was down at most stadiums, and baseball needed a boost. Players liked the idea, too. Fans were allowed to vote for their choice of stars, and they jumped at the opportunity.

A crowd of 49,200 fans paid to see the cream of major league baseball. That first game was won 4–2 by the American League, thanks to a home run by Babe Ruth. From then on, the major league all-star game has been an important and flashy part of professional baseball.

Like everything else in baseball back then, there was another all-star game with a different color. No black played in the first major league all-star game. Jim Crow still made the rules. But blacks had their stars, and they wanted to show them off.

The idea for a Negro league all-star game came from a man named Roy Sparrow in 1932. Sparrow worked for Gus Greenlee in Pittsburgh. Greenlee was always looking for a new event to promote, and a black all-star game was perfect. With Robert Cole, owner of the Chicago American Giants, Greenlee set up the contest for Comiskey Park in August 1933.

They called it the East-West Negro League All-Star Game. Players from the Eastern leagues played those from the Western leagues. Players were elected to the teams by fans who voted with ballots printed in such black newspapers as the *Pittsburgh Courier* and the *Chicago Defender*.

Just like those who organized the first major league all-star game, the men who arranged the first East-West game thought it might take place only once. Instead, it was the start of the most important, best-attended, most glamorous annual event in the history of Negro baseball.

"East meets West!" shouted the headlines. "The Classic of Classics!" Players were ballyhooed in print: "The brilliant Slim Jones!" "The hard-hitting Josh Gibson!" "The colt-like Cool Papa Bell!" The games were called "the most thrilling baseball dramas ever enacted!"

Apart from all the hoopla, the East-West games were great attractions because Negro baseball never had strong enough leagues to hold regular World Series games. With money always a problem and teams going out of business, scheduled games were often cancelled. Many fans were unable to see star players unless they played on strong, sound teams. The fans got that chance with the East-West game. Top individual players could appear no matter how weak their home teams were.

The first game attracted eight thousand fans. That was not an enormous number, especially in comparison with the major league total, but it was a good crowd in the hard times of 1933. Most of the players came from the Pittsburgh and Chicago teams, because most fans voted on the ballots published in the newspapers of those cities. Seven players from the Pittsburgh Crawfords, including Cool Papa Bell, Oscar Charleston, Josh Gibson, and Judy Johnson, played for the East. The Chicago American Giants also sent seven players. The Philadelphia Stars, Homestead Grays, Cleveland Giants, Nashville [Tennessee] Elite Giants, and other teams also sent stars to the contest.

The game was colorful and hotly played. The East was expected to win, but the West took the game, 11–7. Mule Suttles, the Chicago American Giants' big first baseman, clouted a long home run to put the game away. Word spread across black America that the East-West game was the real showpiece of black baseball talent. Soon it was considered *the* game to see.

The 1934 game, played in Comiskey Park in front of twenty-five thousand fans, lived up to its billing. While 1933's contest had been full of hits and runs, the 1934 game had scattered hits and almost no runs. It had good defense. In the fourth inning, Jimmie Crutchfield threw out the hard-hitting Mule Suttles when he tried to score from third on a fly ball. "Mule didn't think Crutchfield had much of an arm," said pitcher Chet Brewer, "and Crutchfield threw him out by ten feet."

The rest of the game was dominated by the pitching of Satchel Paige and Harry Kincannon of the East, and of Teddy "Big Florida" Trent, Chet Brewer, and Willie Foster of the West. For seven innings the game was scoreless.

In the bottom of the seventh inning, Willie Wells of the Chicago American Giants, playing for the West team, doubled.

Wells, a great shortstop, played many years in Mexico, where he got the nickname *El Diablo*, "the devil."

A reporter wrote, "Pandemonium reigned in the West's cheering sections. An instant later a hush fell upon the crowd as the mighty Satchel Paige, 'money' pitcher for the East, leisurely ambled across the field toward the pitcher's box. It was a dramatic moment. Displaying his picturesque double wind-up and nonchalant manner, Satchel started shooting 'em across the plate."

In short order, Paige got the West hitters out.

"This sounded taps for the West, because from then on Sir Satchel was the master of the situation," the newspaper said.

The East went on to win with a run in the eighth inning, scored by Cool Papa Bell.

In 1935, with players from many different teams in the lineups, the game once again was a hitter's parade. Though Jimmie Crutchfield made his famous bare-handed catch, most of the balls went past the fielders. Josh Gibson had four hits in five at bats. With a 4–4 tie after nine innings, the East scored four runs in the tenth to take an 8–4 lead. The West came right back and scored four runs to tie the score in their half of the inning.

That led to the bottom of the eleventh, score tied, the West batting. Martin Dihigo, a crafty pitcher for the New York Cubans, was on the mound. With two men on base and two out, the West's Mule Suttles came to the plate.

What followed was described by William G. Nunn, a young sportswriter for the *Pittsburgh Courier:*

"Dihigo, his uniform dripping with perspiration, wiped the sweat out of his eyes, and shot a fastball across the plate. 'Ball one,' said Umpire Craig.

"Again came that blinding fastball, letter high and splitting

Mule. Not much in the field, George "Mule" Suttles pounded long home runs during a career that lasted from 1918 to 1948. He is shown here in the 1940s.

the plate. And the count was one and one.

"Suttles stepped out of the batter's box, dried his sweating palms in the dust around home plate, tugged on his cap, and moved back into position. He looked dangerous as he wangled his big, black club around. But so did Dihigo, who was giving his all.

"Once again came that smooth motion, that reflex action of the arm, and then!—a blur seeming to catapult towards the plate.

"Suttles threw his mighty body into motion. His foot moved forward. His huge shoulder muscles bunched. Came a swish through the air, a crack as of a rifle, and like a projectile hurled from a cannon, the ball started its meteoric flight. On a line it went. It was headed towards right center. Bell and Gibson were away with the crack of the bat. But so was Arnold, centerfielder of

Pittsburgh Courier *artist George Lee drew the stars of the East-West All-Star game in a cartoon that appeared in the newspaper on the day of the 1937 classic.*

the East team and Oms, dependable and dangerous Cuban star, who patrolled the right garden. No one thought the ball would carry to the stands.

"Headed as it was, it took a drive of better than 450 feet to clear the fence.

Members of the East squad pose shoulder to shoulder before the 1939 East-West classic in Comiskey Park. Forty thousand fans saw them lose to the West, 4–2. Standing (left to right): Buck Leonard, Willie Wells, Rudolfo Fernandez, Sammy T. Hughes, George Scales, Mule Suttles, Pat Patterson, Josh Gibson, Bill Wright, Roy Partlow. Kneeling (left to right): Bill Byrd, Leon Day, Bill Holland, Cando Lopez, Goose Curry, Red Parnell.

"The ball continued on its course and the packed stands rose to their feet. Was it going to be caught?! Was it going to the stands?!

"No, folks! That ball, ticketed by Mule Suttles, CLEARED the distant fence in far away right center, landing 475 feet from home plate. It was a herculean swat. One of the greatest in baseball. As cheering momentarily hushed in the greatest tribute an athlete can ever receive, we in the press box heard it strike the back of a seat with a resounding thud, and then go bounding merrily on its way.

"And then . . . pandemonium broke loose. Suttles completed

Buck. No black player was better year after year than Walter "Buck" Leonard, the Homestead Grays' slugging first baseman. A left-handed line-drive hitter, burly Buck was called the "black Lou Gehrig," after the famous New York Yankee star.

his trip home, the third base line filled with playmates anxious to draw him to their breasts. Over the stands came a surging mass of humanity."

Not every East-West all-star game was that dramatic, but most were just as celebrated. To the players, it was the high point of the season. Many counted it more important to be elected an all-star, even if they sat on the bench, than to play for a winning team back home. White fans and white sportswriters went out of their way to see the game. The spectacle helped open up Negro baseball to a wider audience. Many saw not just great baseball, but the injustice of baseball's color line.

Judy. "A third baseman as good as I ever saw," said Cool Papa Bell about William J. "Judy" Johnson. Called "Jing" by his teammates, Judy was one of the smartest players for Hilldale and the Pittsburgh Crawfords, and was inducted into baseball's Hall of Fame.

Comiskey Park remained the site of the East-West game, because of its size and location. Each year, more fans packed the park. Chicago had many black baseball fans and it was the center of railroad travel. "Chicago was a mecca for blacks from the South," said Jimmie Crutchfield. "When you said in Tennessee or Alabama that you were going to the big city, you meant Chicago."

As the country's economy got better, black fans arranged their vacations around the East-West game. The Union Pacific railroad added more passenger cars to accommodate the travelers.

Not all the games were close and not all of them were played well, but every year the Negro leagues' top stars competed, playing in the uniform of their home team, just as major league all-stars did. The same great players were voted in year after year. Buck

Leonard, the superb first baseman of the Homestead Grays, appeared eleven times. The players posed shoulder-to-shoulder for photographs. They talked to the press. White owners and scouts for major league clubs showed up often. If there was ever a place for a player to show his ability, it was in the East-West games.

And the fans kept coming. Crowds of forty thousand were not uncommon. The 1943 game at Comiskey Park drew a crowd of 51,723, including black entertainers and celebrities. Such popularity moved league officials to schedule a second all-star game later in the year, sometimes in Washington, D.C.'s Griffith Stadium or in New York's Yankee Stadium.

The East-West games also helped league finances. Profits from the games were distributed among Negro league teams, and they helped many weak clubs stay alive. Even players shared the wealth. In the early years the players were not paid, but later they were given $100–$200 each. Many, however, said they would have played in the East-West game for nothing.

"It was an honor to be picked," said Judy Johnson. "It was the glory part of our baseball."

JOSH

Nobody who saw Josh Gibson hit a home run ever forgot it.

Some homers are long fly balls. Some are high flies carried by the wind into the stands. Some are curving line drives that land just fair inside a short fence.

Josh Gibson's home runs, many witnesses said, were *shots*. They were "quick" drives, hit so hard and so long that they were gone before anyone knew it. In some big-league ballparks, Gibson hit balls so hard that they broke the backs of wooden seats in the outfield grandstands. Once, playing in a stadium built next to a prison, he hit a ball over the fence of the ballpark and over the fence of the prison, where it landed in a yard and almost killed an inmate. Another ballpark, in Puerto Rico, had a big tree several feet outside the center field fence. Each time Gibson hit a home run into the tree, a fan climbed up and put a tinsel marker like a

Christmas tree ornament at the spot of the drive. At the end of the season, the tree was dotted with the glittering markers.

Gibson was a bull of a man with thick arms and meaty hands. He may have hit more home runs than any player who ever lived. When smart fans talk of black baseball they first say Satchel Paige. A split second later they say Josh Gibson.

Gibson grew up in Pittsburgh, one of the gritty, industrial Northern cities that drew black workers from the South in the early twentieth century. It was called Steeltown, because its mills turned iron ore into steel for cars, bridges, and skyscrapers. Pittsburgh was also called the Smoky City, because of the mill stacks that belched thick gray smoke from coke furnaces. When the steel mills were going full blast, they produced a haze of smoke that turned day into twilight.

Working in the steel mills was hard and dirty, but it paid well—much better than the wages Mark Gibson was making as a sharecropper in Buena Vista, Georgia. So, in 1921, Gibson left his wife and three children and went to look for work in Pittsburgh. He found it in the huge Carnegie-Illinois Steel plant. Three years later he brought his family up to live with him.

They settled on the North Side of Pittsburgh, a hilly neighborhood full of new arrivals like the Gibson family. Josh, the oldest Gibson boy, loved to run and roller-skate in the hills around his new house. He had been born in 1911, and at thirteen years old, Josh was already big and strong, a fast runner and a natural athlete. He went to the Allegheny Pre-Vocational School, but his heart was not in his studies. He loved winning ribbons in track meets. He was also a fine swimmer.

But it was baseball, a game Josh had played only a little bit in the fields of Georgia, that really captured him. In the crowded streets and parks of Pittsburgh, baseball was played keenly. It wasn't the easy picnic game Josh knew in Georgia, but Josh fit in. His arms strong and muscled, his legs sturdy yet fast, his chest brawny and barreled, Josh swung a baseball bat ferociously. When he connected, the ball screamed off in line drives that tore the stubby mitts off fielders' hands.

Pittsburgh was a center for great baseball played by black and white professional and semi-professional teams, the likes of which Josh would not have seen in rural Georgia. The best black squad was the Homestead Grays, a talented team owned and managed by Cumberland "Cum" Willis Posey. Posey, a college graduate, had been a great player before he took charge of the Grays and made them a powerhouse.

Young men like Josh followed teams like the Grays with much admiration. The top players were role models: adult athletes at their best, men to look up to. Baseball was a livelihood for them, a way to get out of the steel mill and to get paid for doing something they loved.

At sixteen, Josh left school. He had finished only ninth grade, but it was not uncommon for boys his age to quit school and go to work. He found jobs in a department store and in a manufacturing plant. His family needed the money. After work, however, Josh was making a name for himself on North Side ball clubs. He was the top catcher for the Crawford Colored Giants, a good young team that played at Ammon Field. The players were not professionals, but a hat passed among the crowds provided money for equipment and a few dollars for the players. In 1930, fans were asked to pay a nickel to watch. Most could afford only a few pennies.

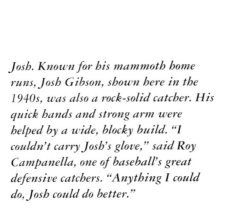

Josh. Known for his mammoth home runs, Josh Gibson, shown here in the 1940s, was also a rock-solid catcher. His quick hands and strong arm were helped by a wide, blocky build. "I couldn't carry Josh's glove," said Roy Campanella, one of baseball's great defensive catchers. "Anything I could do, Josh could do better."

Gibson gave them a show. He was eighteen now, six feet two inches tall, and 190 pounds. There was not a ridge of fat on his body. He hefted four bats at a time, and squeezed the daylights out of the one he chose to hit with. He cracked drives out of ballparks everywhere. Even the *Pittsburgh Courier*, which usually did not cover teams lower than the Grays, wrote about this young slugger "Gipson." Gibson laughed about the misspelling of his name. In years to come, the newspaper would spell it right and spell it often.

The story of how Gibson joined the Homestead Grays has been told so many times that it has become a legend. Legends have many forms, but they often stem from stories whose facts have been changed to make them sound better. The tale puts Gibson in the stands watching a night game between the Grays and the Kansas City Monarchs, in July 1930.

The Grays' pitcher was Smokey Joe Williams, who at fifty-four was still a top attraction. He threw a pitch to Grays catcher Buck Ewing which hit Ewing on the finger and split it. The Grays' other catcher was playing in the outfield and he did not want to catch. Cum Posey spotted Josh in the crowd and asked him if he wanted to catch. "Oh, yeah!" Gibson is supposed to have answered. And for the rest of the night he caught most of what Williams threw. What he missed bounced off his chest, as if Williams were throwing against a wall.

The story is only half true. Buck Ewing was indeed the Grays' catcher, but he was old and Posey was looking for a backup. He had heard plenty about Gibson, and Posey contacted Gibson and told him to be ready to play for the Grays at any time. The Grays were not playing the Monarchs, but a day-night doubleheader against a semi-pro team from Dormont, Pennsylvania. Ewing did split a finger, and Posey put in another catcher until Gibson could be brought over. A taxi picked up Gibson from Ammon Field, where he was playing for the Crawford Giants. A few innings later he was put into the Grays' lineup.

Many years later, Gibson would laugh about the story that had him dropping his hot dogs for a catcher's mitt. But he had become a Homestead Gray. It was mid-1930, he was not even nineteen, and his phenomenal career had begun.

For the rest of the season, Josh Gibson was an important member of the Grays. He took a backseat to older, established players such as Oscar Charleston and Joe Williams, but he watched and learned from them. And, of course, he swung his big bat. In a series of games against New York's strong Lincoln Giants, he swatted several long balls. One of the games was played in Yankee Stadium, Babe Ruth's home park, and Gibson crushed a home run to the bullpen in left field. It landed more than 500 feet away. Fans who saw it would claim that it was one of the longest drives ever hit in that famous stadium.

Such wallops made Josh Gibson a sensation. *Pittsburgh Courier* sportswriters could not say enough about him. They called him the young slugger "who wrecked the Lincoln Giants." They wrote about how strong he was and how much he ate. They wrote about how he wrestled his teammates and easily threw them around. They even dubbed him "Samson" Gibson, after the strongest man in the Bible.

In the years that followed, playing for the Grays, then the Pittsburgh Crawfords, Gibson never let the writers down. It seemed that every one of his home runs left the ballpark, no matter where he was playing, and landed on the pages of the *Courier*. Gibson was a "natural" hitter: it was never necessary to teach him how to hit. He did not swing wildly. Some say he kept his front foot firmly planted and did not lunge at a pitch. Others say he lifted his foot just before he swung, and when infielders saw that foot rise, they backed up in fear.

Much of his power came from the waist up, from his tree-trunk arms and heavy shoulders, and his quick, viselike hands. His swing was controlled, so he usually made contact with the pitch. That is rare for a power hitter. A slugger swings very hard and can be easily fooled by curveballs or off-speed pitches. He often strikes out. Not Gibson. He was a good curveball hitter. In fact, pitchers were warned not to throw Gibson a curveball or a change-up when they got two strikes on him.

People who saw Gibson hit day after day claimed that no one else hit the ball as *hard* as he did. He hit vicious line drives. When he got the ball up, it was gone. Gibson, from the time he was an eighteen-year-old rookie with the Grays, hit home runs. Many of the games were not official, so precise records were not kept, and nobody really knows how many runs Gibson hit. Babe Ruth officially hit 714 home runs. Hank Aaron hit 745. Gibson may have hit more than 1000, but not even Josh himself really knew.

"One year Gibson hit seventy-two home runs that I counted," said Cool Papa Bell, his teammate on the Pittsburgh Crawfords. "He would hit more if all the parks had been fenced in like in the majors. Sometimes the outfielders got back 500 feet and Gibson would still hit the ball over their heads. Have you ever heard of a 500-foot out? But we'd play two, sometimes three games a day and he would be tired and just couldn't run out those long hits."

The stories of his home runs go on and on. Often games were stopped so that the home team could measure a Gibson clout. The mayor of Monessen, Pennsylvania, did so one day, arriving at a distance of 512 feet. One player remembers how Gibson hit a ball so hard at Willie Wells, the great shortstop, that it split the web of skin between the thumb and first finger of Wells's left hand.

He hit them in major league parks such as Yankee Stadium, and in rundown ballfields hard against cornfields. In Washington, D.C.'s Griffith Stadium, then the home of the Washington Senators, his home runs clattered into the upper-deck seats. He once hit three there in one day. In Chicago's Comiskey Park, one of his drives stuck in a loudspeaker perched on top of a fence 435 feet away from home. A groundskeeper had to pry the ball out with his fingers.

He hit four homers in four at bats one day in Zanesville, Ohio. He hit three straight in Fairmont, Virginia. In Indianapolis, one day, a pitcher fooled him with a slow curve. Josh began a hard swing, then stopped and let go of the bat with his left hand. Then, holding the bat only in his right hand, he swatted the ball as if it were a housefly. The ball soared over the fence.

One claim for Gibson's power, however, outdoes them all. Yankee Stadium is so massive, with its outfield bleachers built so high and so far from home plate, that no one, not even Babe Ruth, ever hit a ball completely out of the stadium and onto the street. Josh walloped many there that came close—so close that some people claim he really did hit one out.

Gibson played several games in Yankee Stadium, first against the Lincoln Giants and later against such teams as the Philadelphia Stars and the New York Black Yankees. The games were big attractions and the black newspapers covered them carefully. In 1934, playing against the Stars, Josh is alleged to have hit a home run out of the park. Many black players said they "heard about" the blast, but nobody ever saw it.

Gibson's hitting a ball out of Yankee Stadium was very important to many black players and fans because it was something the great Babe Ruth never did. Throughout his career, Gibson was compared with Ruth. Some sportswriters called Gibson the "black Babe Ruth," although others said Ruth was "the white Josh Gibson." That Gibson may have done something Ruth never accomplished was tantalizing to those who felt that the black slugger never got the credit and fame he deserved.

But Gibson himself never made such a claim. In 1943, when Cum Posey interviewed Gibson about his career for the *Pittsburgh Courier*, Gibson never spoke of such a hit. He mentioned the clout in 1930 against the Lincoln Giants and the blast that stopped the game in Monessen, Pennsylvania—but nothing of putting one out of Yankee Stadium.

To many who played with him, however, Gibson did not need

Decked out and ready to ramble, Josh Gibson, Leroy Matlock, and Jimmie Crutchfield sport caps and "plus fours," the fashion rage of 1934.

to outdo Ruth. Josh was Josh, good enough in his own right.

"I'll never forget some of the balls he hit," said teammate Jimmie Crutchfield. "They went out of the park like the wind."

"It was just such a treat to watch him hit the ball," said Judy Johnson, his friend and teammate.

"The only way you could pitch to him was to throw the ball low and behind him," said Chet Brewer, a frequent opponent.

Brewer was joking, but he was a top pitcher. He knew what pitchers did to home-run hitters like Gibson: they threw at their heads. It is called a "dustback" pitch, or "chin music," or simply a "beanball." The pitch is meant to push big hitters off the plate so they won't clobber the ball so easily. If a batter is hit, a fight often breaks out. In the major leagues today there are strict rules and warnings about dustback pitches.

In Negro league play, however, the rules were much looser and beanballs were common. Gibson was often thrown at, and he never gave an inch. He showed no fear at bat. If he had, pitchers would have whistled chin music at him until he was out of the league. Sometimes he would bend down, pick up a handful of dirt, and look at the pitcher as if to say that he knew what was coming. Then he dug in and terrorized the hurler.

Although Gibson was built to be a catcher, he was not a great one. He was quick for a big man, and he had a good arm, but several other black catchers were rated above him.

"He was a good catcher, too. Smart." said Cool Papa Bell. "He threw a light ball to second. You could catch it bare-handed. Some catchers throw a brick down to second."

He also had hustle, particularly when he was young. He loved the game and was always trying to learn from older players like Judy Johnson. In the hotels or on the bus after a game, Gibson would corner Johnson and say, "Jing?"—Johnson's nickname— "What'd I do wrong today?"

And he seldom got hurt. Catching is a position that often brings injury. Fingers are broken, knees go bad. Foul balls or collisions at home plate can put a catcher out of action for months. Gibson was strong and durable, and he did not wear out. That meant that his bat would be in the lineup. His "murderous bat," people called it.

Like the other stars of his time, Gibson played all over. He had great winter seasons in Puerto Rico. Satchel Paige brought Gibson to the Dominican Republic. He played in many East-West All-Star games and in hundreds of exhibition games against white major leaguers. Every major league team would have loved to have had him in their lineup.

Jimmy Powers, a sportswriter for the *New York Daily News,* wrote in 1939 that Gibson "would be worth $25,000 a year to any club in baseball." Washington Senator pitcher Walter Johnson went better than that. "There is a catcher that any big-league club would like to buy for two hundred thousand dollars. His name is Gibson. . . . He can do anything. He hits the ball a mile. And he catches so easy he might as well be in a rocking chair. Too bad Gibson is a colored fellow."

As good as Gibson was, and as awe-inspiring as his power was, he was not the top attraction in Negro baseball. That honor, of course, went to Satchel Paige. Gibson was quiet and serious, while Paige was a talker and a joker. Gibson silently impressed the fans with his bat; Paige amazed them with his pitching and his personality. The two players were complete opposites. When they played together, the fans were eager to see them both, but it was Paige who left everybody rolling with laughter or shaking their heads.

Gibson never complained about Paige's taking the spotlight. That was not his style. He knew he was no match for Paige's wit and humor. He let his bat do the talking. Sometimes, when they were on opposing teams, they would tease each other, but mostly Josh played seriously.

There is a story about Paige taunting Gibson in a game played in Griffith Stadium in 1942. Before each pitch, Paige is said to have announced that he was going to throw a fastball, each faster than the last. He struck Gibson out with three pitches. It may have happened, but more likely it did not. Paige would not have toyed with Gibson. As much of a showman as Paige was, he had much respect for the silent, proud Gibson.

In interviews over the years, Paige said Josh Gibson was the best hitter in baseball. "You look for his weakness and while you lookin' for it he liable to hit forty-five home runs," Paige said.

Eventually there was an even bigger difference between Paige and Gibson, though. While Paige kept right on playing, Gibson burned out. In 1941, when Gibson was only thirty, he often became dizzy when he went after foul flies. He was still a complete player and his hitting showed no signs of slipping, but his weight went as high as 230 pounds, and his knees began to ache from so many years of squatting behind the plate. He lost much of his base-running speed.

In 1942 he played well but seemed to tire easily. He complained of numbing headaches. To ease the pain he turned to alcohol, usually beer. As a young player, Gibson would eat so much ice cream that his teammates used to joke about it. When the headaches and sore joints came, however, he gave up ice cream in favor of beer. The alcohol seemed to help.

Gibson's problem was hypertension, or high blood pressure, which can be serious if it is not treated. Heavy drinking is especially dangerous for a person with this condition. Gibson was too stubborn to listen when doctors told him to slow down and take care of his health. He had always been as strong as a bull, and he refused to believe he might be a sick man. On New Year's Day, 1943, Gibson lost consciousness and went into a coma. He recovered, but his collapse was a bad sign.

Still, in 1943 Gibson went right back to baseball and led the league in hitting with an incredible .526 average. For the next few years he performed for the Grays and in Puerto Rico. He had always made good money, and at $1500 a month or more, he remained one of the best-paid black players. He walloped homers and made all-star teams even though his coaches knew he had to be rested more often than before. In 1944, however, he hit only six home runs in thirty-nine league games, far fewer than his usual number.

Off the field, Gibson was becoming more ill. He continued drinking. He often had loud fits of anger and times when he was out of control. He threatened suicide and struggled with responding police officers. He was hospitalized and given medicine to calm him, but nothing seemed to help. Many of his teammates worried that Gibson might be using drugs. All of them saw that he was very sick. The robust, happy country boy of a few years ago was now an angry, sullen, dangerous man.

In 1946, when he appeared in his last East-West All-Star game, Gibson was thirty-four. To his fans he looked ten years older. He batted three times and did not hit the ball out of the infield. After the season was over, Ted Page, a former teammate, saw Gibson sitting at the bar in the Crawford Grille in Pittsburgh. Gibson was clutching the collar of a stranger and shaking him violently. Seeing Ted Page, Gibson bellowed, "Tell this man who hit the longest ball anyplace! Tell him!"

That December he turned thirty-five. He was sick and depressed. He saw his career ending. On January 20, 1947, he went to a movie, and while there he suffered a severe stroke. The veins in his brain had ruptured. That night he died in his sleep at his mother's house.

His death shocked all of black baseball. It also made many

Gibson and the Grays. The Homestead Grays were one of the strong teams of Negro baseball. The heart of their 1946 lineup was (left to right) Sam Bankhead, Josh Gibson, Buck Leonard, Dave Hoskins, and Jerry Benjamin. Gibson died only a few months after this photograph was taken.

people very sad. They felt that Josh Gibson had died because, unlike his teammates, he could not handle the reality of his life in baseball. While most Negro league players lived with the hard times and the injustice of the color line, Gibson came to resent them. As the greatest slugger in the game, he was always being told how much he would make in the major leagues and that owners were ready to sign him.

As late as 1942, he had heard those rumors. That year, sports-writers reported that Pittsburgh Pirates owner Bill Benswanger was about to ink Gibson and Buck Leonard. The offer never came. As the years passed, as his health got worse, Gibson became convinced that no major league contract would ever have his name on it. It was too much for him to take.

"He was a big, overgrown boy," Jimmie Crutchfield often said of him. "He was such a *nice* guy. But it bothered him that he wasn't going to make the big leagues. It really did. To me it seems that Josh died of a broken heart."

Crutchfield and Gibson's other teammates missed him. They missed the grinning guy who could hit the ball a mile. Cool Papa Bell had a photo of Gibson with a bat the fans at Griffith Stadium once gave him. On the bat was painted "Josh the Basher."

Said Cool Papa, "I don't care what league or where it was, Josh hit the long ball more often than any other player I've ever seen. Anyone!"

OUR LEAGUES/
THEIR LEAGUES

In 1940 Germany's armies had smashed across Europe, into Poland, and Belgium, and down into France. After storming Norway, Denmark, and Finland, Hitler's Nazi forces looked ready to invade England, America's closest European friend and ally. Some Americans were convinced that Hitler's Nazi forces would even invade the United States. A gun club in Pennsylvania said it was prepared to shoot down any Nazi parachutists descending from the skies.

A debate raged throughout the country over whether or not America was ready to go to war. President Franklin D. Roosevelt was preparing to run for his third term, which presidents could still do then. His most pressing job, however, was to mobilize the country. America's armed forces needed soldiers, equipment, and weapons. The German threat grew worse with each day.

Another problem Roosevelt faced was what people called

America's "Jim Crow Army." Like the rest of American society, the armed forces were divided by color. They had separate units for black and white soldiers. The Navy enlisted blacks solely for jobs in its kitchens and dining halls. Only four blacks had ever graduated from West Point, the army's special officer-training academy. None had ever graduated from Annapolis, the Navy's top school.

Blacks petitioned the President and Congress to provide equal treatment and equal opportunity in the military, especially now that the country was preparing for another world war. From Revolutionary War days, blacks had fought for their country. Now they wanted to do so the same way that white soldiers did.

As war swept Europe and tens of thousands of soldiers were killed, America went on with its daily life. The 1940 baseball season started, and two hundred thousand fans packed into eight major league parks. President Roosevelt threw out the first ball as the Washington Senators played the Boston Red Sox.

The big story on opening day, however, was a no-hitter thrown by a brilliant young pitcher for the Cleveland Indians named Bob Feller. Feller, who was only twenty-one, threw a blinding fastball. His no-hitter was the first ever thrown on an opening day.

Of course, Feller faced no black hitters. None was on the Chicago White Sox, which opposed him, and none was in the major leagues. The color line was holding fast as the new decade began.

Black ballplayers continued their Negro league play and barnstorming tours. Most of the established clubs, such as the Homestead Grays and the Chicago American Giants, were still strong, but many others struggled to stay alive. One that had not made it was the Pittsburgh Crawfords, the most exciting team of the 1930s. The team folded at the end of 1938. Owner Gus

Greenlee had lost a fortune in his business ventures, and the government sued him for unpaid taxes. He was so deeply in debt that he had to sell the team bus. Even Greenlee Field, built only a few years earlier, was torn down. It was a painful blow to Negro baseball, and a loss to fans who had loved the Craws.

Mexico and Latin America also posed a new threat to the Negro leagues. Wealthy owners there were offering contracts so big that more and more top black players, such as Cool Papa Bell, Josh Gibson, and Willie Wells, preferred to perform there rather than on American teams. Their absence hurt Negro league clubs and made them less appealing to fans. Owners like Cum Posey were outraged. They threatened to sue the jumpers and ban them from ever again competing in the Negro leagues.

Of the teams that competed in the Negro National League and the Negro American League, the best in the East were the Homestead Grays, Baltimore Elite Giants, and Newark Eagles. Buck Leonard, the Grays' solid first baseman, was in his prime. Raymond Brown of the Grays was one of the league's best pitchers. With Satchel Paige, the Kansas City Monarchs generally dominated the West.

Besides Paige, the Monarchs' Hilton Smith was recognized as a premier pitcher. Smith was the man who went down in history as Paige's backup. Paige was so famous, he had to appear in almost every game, but he pitched only two or three innings so he would not wear out his arm. The man who usually followed him for the Monarchs was Hilton Smith. He was no easy mark, however, and opponents said Smith's curveball made him one of the game's best hurlers for many years.

The plain fact of the new baseball decade of the 1940s was that black players were no longer a secret. White fans by the thousands

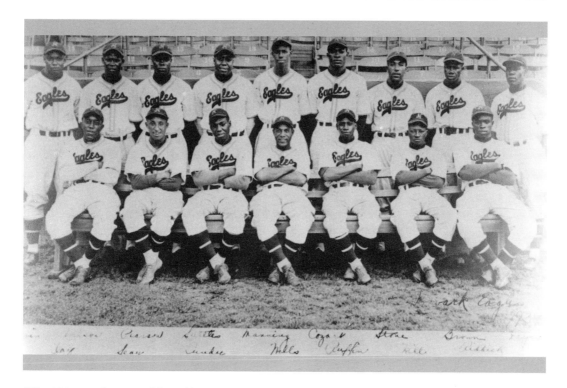

The 1939 Eagles, owned by Effa Manley, were one of several fine Newark teams of the late 1930s and '40s. Their standouts included Monte Irvin (standing, far left) who went on to the major leagues in 1947; Mule Suttles (standing, fourth from left); pitcher Max Manning (standing, fifth from left); pitcher Leon Day (sitting, far left); and infielders Dick Lundy and Willie Wells (sitting, respectively, third and fourth from left).

had seen them play. The *Saturday Evening Post,* a magazine read by millions, ran a full-length feature article on Satchel Paige. *Time* and other news magazines did the same. White owners and managers knew how good blacks were. White major league players had been playing against them for years and could not deny that in many games their black opponents beat their brains out.

Times were changing. The American people were changing. The Depression was loosening its grip. Social attitudes were loosening.

Nearly every family owned a radio and enjoyed entertainment and information from all parts of the country. More and more people owned automobiles, and they traveled the United States as never before. Black performers, singers, jazz artists, and comedians were increasingly popular. *Native Son,* a novel by Richard Wright, a young black from Mississippi, was published and received good reviews. The black heavyweight boxer Joe Louis had been champion of the world for many years. One of the world's most celebrated singers was Marian Anderson, a black woman from Alabama. When she was not allowed to perform at Constitution Hall in Washington, D.C., in 1939, she performed outdoors, in front of the Lincoln Memorial, in a concert that drew one hundred thousand people.

Still, writers in newspapers and magazines referred to race relations as America's "Negro problem." Blacks, after years of separate and unequal treatment in everything from voting rights to drinking fountains, were pushing for fairness. They wanted the basic rights guaranteed them under the Constitution. They wanted an America without separate waiting rooms in train stations and separate entrances at movie theaters. They wanted to be able to go to the public school of their choice. They wanted to be able to get on a bus and sit in any seat that was empty. In many areas of the country in 1940, blacks could still not do any of these things.

The unrest was apparent in baseball. Well-read, respected sportswriters, including Shirley Povich, Heywood Broun, Westbrook Pegler, and Jimmy Powers, continued to complain about the "disgrace." They pointed to many weak, all-white major league lineups when superb black players were available. Powers and other writers liked to dream about how good their favorite teams would be if they could add a Josh Gibson or a Buck Leonard to the lineup.

Shirley Povich wrote in the *Washington Post,* "There's a couple million dollars' worth of baseball talent on the loose, ready for the big leagues. . . . Only one thing is keeping them out of the big leagues—the pigmentation of their skin. They happened to be colored."

In 1940 a magazine called *Friday* asked white major leaguers about black players. Gabby Hartnett, the former star catcher of the Cubs who had become the team manager, said, "If managers were given permission, there'd be a mad rush to sign up Negroes." Leo Durocher, manager of the Brooklyn Dodgers, said he would be in that rush. "Hell, I've seen a million good ones," he said about black players.

So why was the color line not broken? There were many reasons, as many as there were owners, managers, and ballplayers of both colors. One was tradition. Blacks had not been in major league baseball for fifty years—about as long as anyone could remember—and nobody thought to change that. Many white fans admitted years later that they never even noticed that the game was all-white. They just went to games and rooted for their favorites.

Another reason was that baseball teams were private businesses. Even though the public went to the games, the teams and their stadiums were owned by businessmen. In fact, the teams were officially baseball "clubs," and a club allows its members to decide who they want to have belong to it. All the businessmen who owned major-league teams were white, and they thought they knew what their mostly white customers wanted.

After the Black Sox scandal of 1919, owners of major league baseball appointed a commissioner to oversee their leagues. From 1919 to 1944, Judge Kenesaw Mountain Landis, a stern, rigid man, was that commissioner. Landis, a brilliant lawyer, was given credit for cleaning up baseball after the Black Sox gambling scandal. From then on he ruled like a dictator. None of his decisions was ever changed. Everybody in baseball respected him, and most were afraid of him. Even though he stated that "there is no rule, formal or informal, no understanding, subterranean or otherwise," against Negroes players in the majors, he was entirely against it. He never wavered from that position.

As commissioner of baseball, Landis worked for the owners. If they wanted to do something without his permission, they could do so. Yet it would take a strong owner and a strong leader to overrule the commissioner. Very few of them ever tried. In 1943, Bill Veeck, the owner of a minor league baseball team, decided to buy the last-place Phillies and stock it with the best black players in the land. "I had not the slightest doubt that the Phils would have leaped from seventh place to the pennant," said Veeck. Before he made his move, however, he notified Judge Landis. Landis acted quickly and ordered the team sold to somebody else, which it was. Veeck's plan was dashed.

In the meantime, owners came up with flimsy excuses for not signing black players. Most said that the "public" was not ready for it. Ford Frick, then president of the National League, said, "We have always been interested in Negro players but have not used them because of the public. The public has not been educated to the point where they will accept them."

Other white owners said blacks would have a hard time, because many white major leaguers were from the South and would not play with blacks. The owners said blacks would not be welcome in spring training, which mostly took place in the South. They said blacks could not travel with the teams because many hotels would not rent them rooms. Some even said fans would riot if blacks appeared on the field.

All of these claims, of course, were guesses. Most of them were foolish guesses, not borne out by the hundreds of exhibition games in which blacks and whites played with and against one another in front of thousands of spectators, white and black.

Some owners tried to say that the color line served to protect the black players. "A lone Negro in the game will face caustic comments," said Clark Griffith, owner of the Washington Senators, in an interview in a black newspaper. "He will be made the target of cruel, filthy epithets."

The *Sporting News,* which was often called the bible of baseball, agreed with him. The newspaper favored keeping blacks out of major league baseball. Its founder and editor, J. G. Taylor Spink, wrote in 1942, "Clear-minded men of tolerance of both races realize the tragic possibilities and have steered clear of such complications."

But Clark Griffith also knew what he was missing, because he had seen black players perform in his own stadium when the Senators were out of town. In the 1940s the Homestead Grays had made Washington, D.C., with its sizable black population, its second home. Owner Griffith had had to repair the seats that Grays sluggers Josh Gibson and Buck Leonard broke with their line drives.

One Sunday afternoon, Griffith called Gibson and Leonard into his office. Buck Leonard remembered it well: "He asked us, 'Do you fellas want to play major league ball?' 'Yeah, we wanna play major-league ball.' 'Do you think you could make it?' 'Yeah, we thinks we could make it.' 'So, well, I tell ya,' he says, 'if we started takin' colored into the major leagues, we gonna take your best ones and that's gonna break up your league.' I said, 'Well, if that's gonna be better for the players, then it's all right by me.'"

Griffith never acted on his idea. All over the country star black players were having the same kind of conversation with white owners and managers, but in the early 1940s, nothing came of them.

At the same time, black leaders and writers were demanding equal baseball treatment. Articles and editorials in the *Pittsburgh Courier* and the *New York Amsterdam News* argued, scolded, and mocked white owners and officials for their Jim Crow ways. A black can die for his country in wartime, they said, but he cannot run the bases in his country's major leagues.

Most blacks agreed. They wanted to see equal opportunity for their race. Some Negro league owners, however, were not eager to see the color bar broken. If blacks were signed by the major leagues, it would mean the end of their teams and their leagues. They would be out of business, and a few of them were too greedy to give up their profits for the good of the players.

Some black activists urged black ballplayers themselves to get involved, but the activists had little success. Athletes in general do not publicly state their opinions on such issues as race. They seldom lead strikes or protests. Negro league players were no different.

Buck Leonard of the Grays described their attitude. "I remember we played up to Griffith Stadium one Sunday and a group of black protesters was there. And they came in the clubhouse and said they wanted to talk. They said, 'Don't you fellas think you could play in the major leagues?' We said, 'Yeah, we think so.' They said, 'Would you fellas like to play in the major leagues.' 'Yeah, we like to play in the major leagues,' we said. 'So why don't you protest or demonstrate?' they said. We said, 'You fellas demonstrate and protest, we gonna play. We don't have time.' They said, 'Well, aren't you part of the movement?' We said, 'We're part of the game, not the movement. We're part of baseball.'"

By being part of baseball, however, they were part of its color bar.

In November 1944, Commissioner Landis died. The new commissioner was A. B. "Happy" Chandler, the former governor of Kentucky. By this time, America had joined the battle against Germany and Japan in World War II, and thousands of white and black American soldiers were fighting and dying overseas. Commissioner Chandler said, "If a black boy can make it on Okinawa and Guadalcanal [two bloody battle sites], hell, he can make it in baseball." He also said, "I don't believe in barring Negroes from baseball just because they are Negroes."

By 1945, the war had taken many white major-leaguers into the armed services, and major league teams needed new talent. At the same time, crowds at Negro league games were bigger than ever. Many fans were turned away from the East-West All-Star games at Comiskey Park because the stadium was packed.

There were many reports of tryouts for black players before major league scouts and managers. Most of the prospects were young, inexperienced Negro league players.

In Chicago, Jimmy Dykes, the manager of the White Sox, held a tryout for two young Kansas City Monarchs players, Nate Moreland, a pitcher, and Jackie Robinson, an infielder. Dykes thought the two were very good. "Personally I'd welcome them," Dykes said. But he was not given permission to sign them.

Moreland was very bitter. "I can play in Mexico," he said, "but I have to fight for America where I cannot play."

Wendell Smith, a leading writer for the *Pittsburgh Courier*, brought three players—Jackie Robinson, Sam Jethroe of the Cleveland Buckeyes, and Marvin Williams of the Philadelphia Stars—for a tryout in Boston. They played in front of Boston Red Sox manager Joe Cronin and coach Hugh Duffy. Cronin and Duffy said they were impressed, but, again, no contracts were offered.

Two older players, pitcher Terris McDuffie and first basemen Dave "Showboat" Thomas, were also looked at, by the Brooklyn Dodgers. Both men had played for many Negro league teams, but McDuffie was thirty-six and Thomas was thirty-nine. They were too old to perform well.

Even though none of these tryouts resulted in the breaking of the color line, the foundation was being laid. People were looking. Almost everybody could feel a change in the air. It was almost as if they were waiting for one strong, remarkable person to step across the line and strike down Jim Crow.

At the end of the 1945 season, they would not have to wait long.

JACKIE

Jackie Robinson.

He was a chunky guy with thick arms and legs. Some people even called him fat. He had a large head and a full face. He wore his cap back high on his head with the bill up so it looked as if it was too small for him. He had a great smile, when he smiled. Most often he had a fierce look of concentration, his dark eyes blazing.

Jackie Robinson.

When he walked his feet were pigeon-toed, or turned in. The same people who thought he was overweight were certain he was a slow runner. He took little steps to start, but after three or four he was sprinting full out.

Quicker than you can say Jack Robinson.

He hit the ball to right. He pulled it to left. He laid down a bunt. On first base he took big lead-offs and dared the pitcher to pick him off. He stole bases with barreling slides or artful sweeps in which his toe would just catch the edge of the bag. He even stole home—something almost never seen today—and he did it several times.

Jackie Robinson.

Some people called him baseball's "great experiment." To Jackie Roosevelt Robinson, however, it was a chance. He was a black man in a white man's league. He was a ballplayer, and for him that was not an experiment, but a sure thing.

Except that in 1946, with millions—many of whom desperately wanted him to fail—watching his every move, nothing was a sure thing. He had to show proof of his ability. He had to represent his race. He had to match the talent of all those great Negro league players who never had a chance.

Few men or women, in or out of baseball, have ever had so much riding on their shoulders.

Jackie Robinson.

Branch Rickey was one of baseball's smartest men. He had a college degree and he had once been a schoolteacher. He had bushy eyebrows and wore bowties, two things that made him look more like a school principal than a baseball executive. He also had a fine vocabulary. One of his nicknames was Mahatma, after Mahatma Gandhi, India's great leader. But Rickey's intelligence went further than what he had learned in school. He was a man able to see what others did not. He knew how to plan and how to change things for the better.

Working for the St. Louis Cardinals in the 1930s, Rickey had created baseball's minor league or "farm system." His idea was to have a major league team sign contracts with a group of minor league teams. A young player would be assigned to one of these "farm" teams so he could develop. As he got better he would move up to teams in better leagues, until he was ready for the parent teams in the majors. It was a brilliant idea, and the Cardinals became one of the strongest teams in baseball.

In 1942 Rickey was president and general manager of the Brooklyn Dodgers. He was fair as well as intelligent, and he felt that the color line was not only wrong, but stupid. A good baseball team should get the best players possible, he believed, no matter what their color.

Almost every baseball fan at the time had a theory about why Branch Rickey wanted to sign a black player after all the years of Jim Crow. Some said it was only for money: Good players make winning teams. Winning teams make money. Baseball is a business, and money, of course, has always been the prime reason for any changes in business. And Rickey always said he was a good businessman.

David Malarcher, a top black player and longtime manager of the Chicago American Giants, often said, "We are going to be admitted to the major leagues when we can take something to the major leagues in money. Through the years we did not have the kind of patronage that the major leagues thought much of. Finally, we started the East-West All-Star games. The major leagues saw those fifty thousand people out there in that ballpark.

"Branch Rickey had something else in mind than just a little colored boy. He had those great crowds. That is what did it. He realized blacks could bring money to the game."

Rickey also believed, however, that the integration of major league baseball was right. Many years earlier he had been the coach of a college baseball team in Ohio. He brought his team to South

Bend, Indiana, to play Notre Dame. At a local hotel, his catcher, Charley Thomas, was refused a room because he was black. Thomas, Rickey said later, was stunned. "I sat and watched him, not knowing what to do, until he began tearing at one hand with the other—just as if he were trying to scratch the skin off his hands with his fingernails. I was alarmed. I asked him what he was trying to do to himself.

"'It's my hands, Mr. Rickey. They're black. If only they were white, I'd be as good as anybody then.'"

Rickey responded, "Charley, the day will come when they won't have to be white."

As president of the Dodgers, Rickey held fast to that statement. "I couldn't face my God any longer," he said, "knowing that his black children were held separate and distinct from his white children in a game that has given me all I own."

His words were followed by actions. In January 1946, major league owners and league officials wrote a secret report on the possibility of blacks breaking the color line. The report forcefully recommended that they not be allowed into the major leagues. A vote was taken and passed, 15–1, in favor of keeping blacks out. The only vote against was Branch Rickey's.

A year earlier, in 1945, Rickey had set up a team called the Brooklyn Brown Bombers. It was a black team playing in the newly formed all-black United States Baseball League. The Brown Bombers would use Brooklyn's Ebbets Field when the Dodgers were out of town. The arrangement was no different than those many black teams had had for years. Rickey could use the Brown Bombers to look at the best black players and determine which one should become the first to break the color line.

The Brown Bombers were managed by the veteran star Oscar

Charleston. Other teams in the new league were from Chicago, Toledo, Philadelphia, and Detroit. An important man in the league was Gus Greenlee, the former Pittsburgh Crawfords owner, who wanted to get back into black baseball.

In looking for a good player to be the first modern black major-leaguer, Rickey had to make the hardest of any baseball decision. It was hard for many reasons. How old should the player be? Were great players like Josh Gibson, Satchel Paige, and Cool Papa Bell—by then in their mid- to late-thirties—too old? But, if a young, unproven player was signed, would he be able to perform well while facing so much attention and pressure? Should a pitcher be signed? Or a home-run hitter? Should it be a player from the South or the North? And what about his personality? A great but feisty player might be goaded into fighting. On the other hand, a soft-spoken player might not have the fire to play hard.

To make his decision, Rickey had to rely on the advice of his scouts, older men, usually former players, who traveled all over the country looking for new talent. The scouts suggested several players to Rickey. Dan Bankhead was a good young pitcher. Roy Campanella was a solid catcher for the Baltimore Elite Giants. Piper Davis was a strong player for the Birmingham Black Barons. Sam Jethroe and Marvin Williams were top players.

By 1945, the Negro leagues had been in operation in one form or another for a quarter of a century. Some of their greatest stars were dead; others were showing considerable gray hair. Black baseball aged its players quickly because, with no off-season, they had to play so many games, travel so many miles in rickety buses, and sleep in a legion of lumpy beds.

Yet many older black players so loved the game that they could not think of doing anything else. Some had remarkably

Campanella. After Roy Campanella went to Brooklyn from the Baltimore Elite Giants in 1946, the Dodgers won five pennants in Campy's ten seasons. A great catcher and a clutch hitter, Campanella was named the National League's Most Valuable Player three times.

long careers. Smokey Joe Williams first pitched at age nineteen in 1897 and he was still throwing in 1932—thirty-five years later! Oscar Charleston, a player and then a player-manager from 1915 to 1950, also had a thirty-five-year career. Others, such as Buck Leonard, Cool Papa Bell, and, of course, Satchel Paige, had played two decades or more and were still active when Branch Rickey was looking for his pioneer player.

The general belief was that the perfect candidate to break the color line would be a solid performer on a Negro league team— maybe a six-year veteran, a consistent .300 hitter with good power and run production. A Buck Leonard, the clutch-hitting first baseman, would be perfect. Or a proven pitcher with the great speed of Joe Williams and the control and savvy of Satchel Paige.

Nobody thought big leagues would sign a Negro league rookie. But that is what Branch Rickey did on October 23, 1945, when he offered a major league contract to a first-year player from the Kansas City Monarchs named Jackie Roosevelt Robinson.

Robinson was born in Cairo, Georgia, during the great flu epidemic of 1919. He was the youngest of five children, and his father left the family six months after his birth. His mother, Mallie, moved the family to Pasadena, California, where they lived with Jackie's uncle. Mallie Robinson worked as a domestic, a person who cleans house and washes for others. She moved the family into a little rented house on Pepper Street.

Jackie grew up looking for trouble. He ran with a gang of boys in his neighborhood who called themselves the Pepper Street Gang. Yet although they often stole and did damage, the gang also played sports. Soon Jackie was the best at baseball, basketball, football, even golf. He was a natural athlete.

At the same time his older brother, Mack, was making a name for himself. Mack was a terrific sprinter. At Pasadena Junior College he set records in the sprint and the long jump. In the 1936 Olympic Games in Munich, Germany, Mack represented the United States and came in second in the 200-meter dash. He lost to the American runner Jesse Owens.

Jackie followed Mack to Pasadena and even broke some of Mack's track records at the school. He also starred on the baseball, basketball, and football teams. He matured into a true athlete/scholar. From the junior college he went to the University of California at Los Angeles. He was successful there, particularly in football. He became one of the best college running backs in the nation. He was able to start, stop, and change directions so quickly that tacklers were left grabbing at air.

Just as in junior college, Robinson played four sports at UCLA. He was a superb athlete—maybe the top overall athlete in America. Then the United States entered World War II. Before he could graduate, he was drafted into the army.

It was at Camp Hood, Texas, that Robinson showed how much spirit and pride he possessed. The army was not as fair in its treatment of blacks as college had been. When the driver of a city bus told him to sit in the back, Robinson refused. He insisted on his right to sit where he wanted. The argument escalated, until his commanding officer became involved.

Robinson was charged with conduct unbecoming to an officer and was tried in military court. If he was found guilty, he would be dishonorably discharged. Robinson was found innocent, but the episode marked him. On one hand, he knew he could not back down from what was right. On the other hand, fighting for his rights could cause trouble.

After he left the army in 1945, Robinson signed on to play for the Kansas City Monarchs for $400 a month. Many of the Monarch players were veterans of the Negro leagues and of years of barnstorming, and they were not impressed with Robinson's college successes. This was black baseball, and he had to prove himself.

Jimmie Crutchfield was thirty-five when he played against Robinson that spring. "I remember seeing Jackie for the first time. He was fat," Crutchfield later said. "And I thought the Monarchs had him just for a publicity stunt because he had been so great in college. We were playing an exhibition game in Houston, Texas, and Jackie hit a ball between the third baseman and the bag down the left-field line. Our left-fielder ran over and got the ball quickly

The legend and the pioneer. Satchel Paige jaws with Jackie Robinson in 1945, his teammate on the Kansas City Monarchs. At the end of that season, Robinson signed with the major league Brooklyn Dodgers.

and wheeled it into second. But Jackie was standing on the bag. He was already there. I knew right then the guy could move. We were together for about six or seven games that spring, and during that time we couldn't get him out."

Although Robinson played well for the Monarchs, he was not their star. Many players would later say that the Monarchs had better performers. What he was best at, however, was complaining. He did not like the life of black baseball. He did not like many of the bad fields they played on, nor the "low salaries and sloppy umpiring." He did not like the traveling, the bad food, the uniforms that often went days without being washed. He did not like that the rooms were "dingy and dirty" and the "hotels of the cheapest kind."

Robinson did not smoke or drink, and he disapproved of some

of the Monarchs who went on after-hours binges. All in all, he did not fit in well. Through the years, his teammates had grown to accept Negro league conditions and they felt he should, too. He was lonely and angry. He often got into shouting matches off the field, and into scuffles with opponents on the field. At one time he wanted to quit the Monarchs, but the team owner, J. L. Wilkinson, gave him a raise in pay, and Robinson agreed to stay.

He played hard. He never gave his opponents an edge.

"He was fiery in our league. He was out to win every day," said Jimmie Crutchfield.

He was also smart. He knew the game. He used his brains and speed to get a split-second advantage out of any situation. What he did not know was that Clyde Sukeforth, a scout for Branch Rickey, president of the Brooklyn Dodgers, was watching him closely.

On August 28, 1945, Rickey asked Sukeforth to bring Robinson to his office in Brooklyn. Robinson thought he was going to be offered a job on the Brooklyn Brown Bombers. He was twenty-six years old, and he was looking for something better than the Monarchs.

What followed was a remarkable meeting. There was the bow-tied, bushy-browed Rickey, smoking a cigar and speaking in lofty phrases with wild gestures. There was the thick-set, intense Jackie Robinson, the college star and Negro league ballplayer who seldom took grief from anyone. The conversation lasted close to three hours.

"Do you know why I asked Clyde to bring you to see me?" Rickey asked.

Robinson said he thought it concerned the Brown Bombers.

"No," said Rickey, "I think you can play in the major leagues. You were brought here to play for the Brooklyn organization, perhaps, as a start, for Montreal."

With a shake of a black hand in a white one, Jackie Robinson and Branch Rickey of the Brooklyn Dodgers break baseball's color line on October 23, 1945.

He then spoke for a long time, telling Robinson that he knew all about him and about what a competitor he was. He knew about his trouble in the army. He knew about Robinson's temper.

"Mr. Rickey," Robinson finally said, "are you looking for a Negro who is afraid to fight back?"

"No," Rickey said, "I'm looking for a ballplayer with guts enough *not* to fight back!"

Robinson signed. That winter he got married to Rachel Isum, a girl he had met at UCLA, and he played winter ball in Venezuela. The next spring he reported to Montreal to play for the white, minor league Royals. Finally, in 1946, the "great experiment" had begun.

In his very first game Robinson got four hits in five at bats. He hit a homer and drove in four runs. He stole two bases and scored four runs. Once, on third base, he danced and faked, causing the

"Now batting: Zha-kee Robinson." Jackie Robinson in his historic first at bat as a member of the minor league Montreal Royals in 1946. The day the color bar was broken, Robinson got four hits, and the Royals beat Jersey City, 14–1.

opposing pitcher to interrupt his motion and balk, a move that allowed Robinson to move up a base and score. His *mostly* white Royals won 14–1.

To the many French fans in Montreal, Robinson became "Zha-kee." They were wild about him. He returned the favor by hitting .349, the top average in his league. He also stole forty bases.

As Robinson had been warned, it was not easy. Opponents tried to make him fail. He could not respond to taunts from other players or from fans in other cities. He could not fight back when he was thrown at or spiked by runners sliding into second base. He had to turn the other cheek.

The pressure kept him up at night. He did not eat well. He was so nervous that his wife worried that he might break down.

The worst abuse came during the league play-offs against the Louisville, Kentucky, team. Their players and fans were unmerciful. They called Robinson every racial name they could think of. And it worked. He hit badly and the Royals lost the first two games.

Back in Montreal, however, the fans decided to make up for the rotten treatment Robinson had received. They chanted, "Zha-kee! Zha-kee!" when he came up to bat. "Zha-kee" replied by going on a tear and leading the Royals to three victories and the championship. After the final game, Royals players and fans lifted Jackie on their shoulders and carried him off the field. "It was the greatest thing that ever happened to me," Robinson said.

Greater things were to happen, but not without further trials. When they arrived at spring training in 1947 with the Brooklyn Dodgers, in Florida, Jackie and Rachel found that taxis would not pick up them up. Hairdressers would not work on Rachel's hair. Rachel had to enter some ballparks through a "colored" entrance far in the outfield. Branch Rickey had said it would not be easy, and it was not.

Still, in 1947 Robinson started for the Dodgers in Ebbets Field. It had been almost sixty years since a black man—Moses Fleetwood Walker—had played in the major leagues. Jackie Robinson, Branch Rickey's pioneer, changed the face of baseball. On opening day, 1947, with a skip out to his position at second base and a smile that masked the hottest determination of any man alive, Jackie Robinson smashed baseball's color line.

THE DEATH OF
JIM CROW

The walls that kept blacks out of major league baseball did not come tumbling down. They were taken apart brick by brick. Jackie Robinson's success in 1946 at Montreal did not move white owners to run out and sign dozens of Robinsons for their clubs. First came one black ballplayer, then two, then a few others. Some teams waited several years before they signed a black player. The New York Yankees had none as late as 1954. The Boston Red Sox waited until 1959.

But Robinson was not a lone pioneer. The minor league Montreal Royals also signed John Wright, a pitcher who had played with several Negro league teams. Wright was not one of the aces of the black leagues, certainly not a Satchel Paige nor a Chet Brewer, but at age twenty-seven he was a solid, proven hurler.

Wright did not last long with the Royals. He did not pitch

well, and after a few appearances he was sent to a lower minor-league team. Jackie Robinson said that the pressure was too much for his black teammate. Wright felt that he had to show that he deserved to be one of the first blacks in white baseball, and he tried too hard.

"John had all the ability in the world," said Robinson. "But John couldn't stand the pressure of going up into this new league and being one of the first. . . . He tried to do more than he was able to do."

Two other black players were signed by the Dodgers in 1946. One was the Baltimore Elite Giants' hard-hitting catcher Roy Campanella, and the other was a young black pitcher from the Newark Eagles named Don Newcombe. They were both sent to a minor league team in New Hampshire and were not expected to move up as fast as either Robinson or Wright.

Every time a black player was signed, black newspapers wrote long, proud stories about him. Robinson's stupendous first game with the Royals made headlines in the black press. The papers covered every game in which black players performed. Blacks all over the country wanted to know how the experiment was coming. At the same time, the publicity put even more pressure on the players.

During this period, the Negro leagues were still in operation and more successful than ever. World War II had ended in 1945, and America was experiencing much better times economically. Fans were showing up in big numbers to see Negro league teams at home and when they barnstormed. There were two East-West All-Star games in 1946, one held in Washington, D.C., the other the traditional game, held in Comiskey Park. The game at Comiskey drew 45,474 patrons. While many of the players were new, fresh talents, some of the old stars still made the lineups.

The Other Pioneer. Pitcher Johnny Wright, a veteran of the Homestead Grays with a great assortment of curve balls, was signed to the minor league Montreal Royals just a few months after Jackie Robinson. Although some thought he was a better prospect than Robinson, Wright never made it to the major leagues.

Playing for the West were such veterans as Alex Radcliffe, the brother of Ted "Double Duty" Radcliffe. Quincy Troupe, a fine catcher who had played for the Homestead Grays and the Chicago American Giants, was also on the squad. On the East team was the great Buck Leonard, who was still playing for the Grays. Josh Gibson made an appearance. There were Sam Bankhead, who had played with Gibson on the Crawfords and Grays; Howard Easterling of the Grays; and Henry Kimbro, a fine outfielder from the Baltimore Elite Giants.

Because the teams were drawing more fans than ever before, the players were better paid than they had ever been. Satchel Paige was said to be making as much as $7000 a month! Josh Gibson and Buck Leonard each earned $1500 a month.

There was an odd thing about these Negro league salaries. Jackie Robinson, John Wright, and the other black players who had signed into the white minor league teams earned less than if they had stayed with the Negro league teams. Robinson's $400 a month from the Royals was $200 less than what the Monarchs would have paid him. The real payoff, of course, was to come later.

In the meantime, white owners had their eyes on other black prospects. They were watching the Newark Eagles' Larry Doby, Monte Irvin, and pitcher Leon Day. They liked Philadelphia's Bus Clarkson and Baltimore's Sammy Hughes. Others being considered were Roy Welmaker and Jerry Benjamin of the Grays, Sam Jethroe of Cleveland, Piper Davis of Birmingham, and Verdel Mathis of Memphis.

The great names of the Negro leagues were not on the list. Josh Gibson, Satchel Paige, Cool Papa Bell, Buck Leonard—all were considered too old to go through the minor leagues. Many owners felt these players would not accept the abuse they would get from fans in small towns. Amazingly enough, no owner considered signing one of these stars and putting him directly on a major league team. It had taken sixty years to go this far, and it was as if nobody was going to be rushed.

That decision seemed silly in light of how well the old black pros did against major league opponents. In the winter of 1946, Satchel Paige put together an all-star team—appropriately named Satchel Paige's All-Stars—and barnstormed with white all-star teams. Most of the travel was by car, but the team made some trips in a plane called *Flying Tiger*. That was a luxury for men who had spent lifetimes riding rattletrap buses.

Besides Satchel himself, his all-stars included his back-up ace on the Monarchs, Hilton Smith; veterans Buck O'Neil and Frank Duncan of the Monarchs; Cleveland's Quincy Troupe and Sam Jethroe; the Grays' Howard Easterling; and several other good young players.

In October they went against a major league all-star team headed by Bob Feller of the Cleveland Indians. With Feller were such players as Phil Rizzuto of the Yankees, Johnny Sain of the

Monte Irvin, shortstop, and Larry Doby, second baseman, of the Newark Eagles. When Cleveland Indians owner Bill Veeck signed Doby in 1947, Eagles owner Effa Manley offered him Irvin's contract for just a thousand dollars more. Veeck refused because he thought Irvin was too old. "Shows you how smart I was," said Veeck later. Irvin went to the New York Giants instead, played against Doby in the 1954 World Series, and is in baseball's Hall of Fame.

Braves, and Bob Lemon and Ken Keltner of the Indians. In eleven tough, close games, the Feller team won six and lost five.

The black stars enjoyed watching their major league foes put up with life on the touring circuit. The tough conditions were quite a jolt for them.

"The big leaguers that started barnstormin' with us, they couldn't understand it to save their life," said Paige. "They would have to go in cars. They been layin' up in their feather beds, trainin', and when they began to ride those cars and keep up with us playin' ball, they couldn't do it. They wanted to know how in the *world* we did it so long. Can't stretch your legs out in four or five hours. They never heard such a thing."

The results of the games made it obvious that black stars such as Paige could step in and compete against established major-leaguers. They did not need to prove themselves in the minor leagues. Still, none of them was signed for the top clubs.

Satchel Paige was not even modest when he talked about it.

"It looked like I shoulda got first preference," he said. "But I didn't. That makes you feel a little rough about it at times."

But Jackie Robinson blazed a trail in 1947. He was everything a ballplayer, rookie or otherwise, black or white, could be. He batted .297 and was named National League Rookie of the Year. The Dodgers won the National League pennant.

In July of that year, Larry Doby was signed off the Newark Eagles to play on the Cleveland Indians. He became the first black in the American League. More black players were signed that year, some taken right into major league teams, others going into the minor leagues.

The door was now ajar and opening wider. Still, things were not easy for the black faces who appeared on white minor- and major-league fields. The same racial prejudice that kept the color bar in place was there when it was broken. Black players confronted the old hatred and bigotry, from players and fans alike. It was crude and mean, and it hurt. The word *nigger* was shouted at them, or hissed at them, or silently mouthed. Some black players said it was so common they did not even hear it anymore. Others said they heard it every time.

Roy Campanella, who came up to the Dodgers a year after Jackie Robinson, remembered the treatment well.

"Truthfully, when Jackie and I come into the major leagues there was very few good things said from any of our opposition. And even from some of our teammates," said Campy. "One player insisted that he'd rather pick cotton than play with a colored ballplayer. We had all kind of remarks thrown at us.

"Some players let the ball talk for them. The pitchers, they would throw at you a lot. It got so that they were ashamed to holler at you, but when you'd come to bat the pitcher would throw at your head.

"One day I was batting in Milwaukee. Now Lew Burdette is a

Larry Doby of the Newark Eagles, signing a major league contract with Cleveland Indians owner Bill Veeck. On July 3, 1947, Doby became the first black to play in the American League. A year later, Doby helped the Indians win the world championship. "When Doby hit a tremendous home run to put us ahead in the fourth game of the World Series," wrote Veeck, "it could be observed that none of the 81,000 people who were on their feet cheering seemed at all concerned about—or even conscious of— his color."

great guy, but when I come to bat he knocked me down on the first pitch. I didn't mind. I got up again. On the next pitch he knocked me down again. So okay, that's two. So I got up again, I wasn't too mad. The next time he knocked me down again and I went out to the mound after him. I didn't mind bein' thrown at, but three times in a row, I wouldn't accept that."

Even when Campanella, Robinson, and Don Newcombe paced the Dodgers to the 1949 World Series, they had to face racial insults.

"In the World Series against the Yankees and Casey Stengel," said Campanella, "I'll never forget this, Casey said, 'Stick one in that nigger's ear.' It happened to be a fastball and I stuck it right up in the left-field seats."

Campanella then said something that was true of every black player in the major leagues in those early years: "If I had let those things bother me I wouldn't have been successful."

Jackie Robinson's playing got better and better, but he did let those things bother him. He had his share of run-ins and hard plays. While he tried to live up to Branch Rickey's demand that he not fight back, he never backed down from anybody who came after him.

"Adventure. Adventure. The man is all adventure," said Branch Rickey about Robinson. "I only wish I could have signed him five years sooner."

In 1948, with several black players in the major leagues and more being signed every day, Satchel Paige, who was almost forty-two years old, wanted his shot. After Larry Doby was signed by the Indians, Paige sent a telegram to Bill Veeck, the Indians' owner. "Is it time yet?" Paige wired. Veeck, who had seen Paige pitch many times and thought he was sensational, answered, "All things in due time."

The very next season Veeck's Indians were making a run for the pennant and Satchel's time was due. That July, near Paige's forty-second birthday, Veeck signed him off the Kansas City Monarchs. Paige joined the Indians' pitching staff. Finally, the two worlds of baseball had been fully joined. The greatest name of the Negro leagues was wearing a major league uniform.

How much did Satchel Paige's appearance in the major leagues mean to black fans? That was shown on the night of August 20, 1948, in Chicago's Comiskey Park. Paige was announced as the starting pitcher against the White Sox. A big crowd was expected. Nobody, however, had expected such a throng. Comiskey Park held 61,000 fans, but so many fans, black and white, showed up that ticket takers could not handle the demand. The crush of fans ripped the turnstiles right out of the concrete. When the game began, a crowd estimated at seventy-one thousand people was jammed inside the stadium. Thousands more crowded on the sidewalks outside.

Even Paige admitted he was nervous at such a mob, but he pitched his forty-two-year-old heart out and allowed only three

Newk. Young Don Newcombe of the Newark Eagles was only twenty when the Brooklyn Dodgers grabbed him in 1946. The big fastballer came through for the Bums in the 1950s, winning at least twenty games in three different seasons.

hits and no runs. Even though the Indians had beaten the home team White Sox, the fans roared and stomped their feet with love and admiration for Paige.

While Paige, Robinson, Doby, and others were doing themselves proud in the major leagues, by 1947 the Negro leagues were floundering. Attendance was down. Fans would travel hours to see Robinson and the others, but they would not walk down the street to see black teams.

"We couldn't draw flies," said Buck Leonard.

Forty-two thousand turned out for the 1948 East-West game, but many said that was because fans wanted to see which black players were headed for the major leagues. Even strong Negro league teams like the Homestead Grays were losing money. Black newspapers wrote more about blacks in the majors than they did about the remaining black teams. Many teams went on the road and relied on clowning and other gimmicks to draw fans. The Indianapolis Clowns signed a woman to their team.

Many teams, such as the Newark Eagles, made money selling their top young players to the major leagues. In doing that, however, the team owners knew they were preparing for the end of Negro baseball. They sold such players as Ernie Banks, Willie Mays, Monte Irvin, Jim Gilliam, and Joe Black. These were sparkling players—the new Bells, Gibsons, and Paiges—and they became great major-leaguers.

With their best players in the white leagues, the owners of Negro league teams knew they would soon be out of business. As crowds grew thinner, they could not afford to pay their players. Salaries, so high at the beginning of the 1940s, were now almost nothing.

The year 1950, the beginning of the second half of the twentieth century, would mark the last season for the Negro American League. One by one, the teams went out of business and hung up their uniforms for good. The Indianapolis Clowns won the Eastern Division. (Two years later the Clowns would sign an eighteen-year-old player named Henry Aaron, who would play for them a few months before going into the majors and setting the all-time home run record.) The Kansas City Monarchs, with shortstop Ernie Banks, another future major league star, won the West. The last East-West All-Star game was played in 1950.

Only a few black barnstorming teams kept playing. Some would tour and entertain for many years to come. People still loved them, and they were a great attraction, particularly in small towns. But they were now carryovers, a reminder of things past.

The action, indeed, the future for all players black and white, was in major league baseball. Even though many major league teams would stay all-white for years, the color line had been broken. Jim Crow was not dead, but he was dying. The proud, ragged, remarkable Negro league teams, once the only place a black man could play the game of baseball, were no longer necessary.

OLD-TIMERS

When their leagues were finished, black ballplayers who were not signed by major league teams went back to quiet, ordinary lives. They had spent every waking hour pursuing a game. Now they returned to their families and had to seek regular jobs.

Few of them had any money. Apart from baseball, few had any skills or education. Most took jobs as janitors, postal workers, security guards, or factory workers. Ted Page ran a bowling alley in Pittsburgh. Jack Marshall became a fine bowler and started a bowling pro shop in Chicago. David Malarcher sold insurance and real estate in Chicago, and he also was a poet. Willie Foster became dean of men and baseball coach at Alcorn College in Mississippi.

Baseball put some to work. Satchel Paige was usually doing something for some team. He left the major league St. Louis

Browns in 1953. After that he barnstormed for the Monarchs and other teams. He would take the mound, throw to a few hitters, and, as always, entertain the crowd with his chatter. With a co-author he wrote his life story, called *Maybe I'll Pitch Forever*. Almost everybody knew him. A producer in Hollywood gave him a part in a western movie.

But even Satchel had some hard times. When he could not find a team to run with, he looked for work like anybody else. For a while he was a deputy sheriff in Kansas City. Often he was out of work and out of money.

In 1968 he joined the Atlanta Braves as a pitcher and coach. He was sixty-two years old, but he still thought he had the stuff to pitch.

"I got bloopers, loopers, and droopers," Satchel said. "I got a jump ball, a screwball, a wobbly ball, a hurry-up ball, a nothin' ball, and a bat dodger."

Still, his time on the Braves qualified him for a major-league retirement pension, which was a big help to him and his family.

Other former black stars could not entertain like Satchel, but they did stay in baseball. Judy Johnson, Ted "Double Duty" Radcliffe, Chet Brewer, Ray Dandridge, and others became scouts for major league teams. Buck O'Neil, a top first baseman for the Kansas City Monarchs, scouted and signed Ernie Banks and Lou Brock to major league clubs. O'Neil also coached for the Chicago Cubs.

As the years passed, young black players became as much a part of major league baseball as electric scoreboards and trading cards. By the middle of the 1950s, baseball's top stars—Jackie Robinson, Roy Campanella, Willie Mays—were black. Fans began to take their presence for granted. Negro league players were forgotten.

The players discovered that the young people in their communities knew nothing about Negro baseball. This made the former players sad and a little angry.

Negro league veterans were not selfish or boastful men, but they felt they should be recognized for what they had done. Young people, they complained, too often think that everything started with them. Some baseball historians suggested that baseball's Hall of Fame, the official museum of baseball lore, should include the greatest Negro league stars.

In 1966, a boost came from an unexpected source. Ted Williams—the Boston Red Sox hitter who, some say, may have been the greatest natural hitter ever—accepted his place in the Hall of Fame and said, "I hope that someday Satchel Paige and Josh Gibson will be voted into the Hall of Fame as symbols of the great Negro players who are not here only because they were not given a chance to play."

Many black veterans thought Williams's statement opened people's eyes. Articles and news reports began to appear about Cool Papa Bell, Satchel Paige, and other players. They were called "living legends." In 1970 a book titled *Only the Ball Was White,* by Robert Peterson, was published. It was the first complete history of the Negro leagues. It contained many photographs, facts, personal stories, and hard-to-find statistics of black baseball from its beginnings.

Suddenly, former black players were discovered all over again. In 1971, the Hall of Fame announced that it would appoint a committee to choose Negro league stars worthy of honor. At first the Hall of Fame wanted to set up a separate section for Negro league stars. Many complained that this would be yet another form of racism, just like putting blacks in the back of the bus. Finally it was decided that a special committee would recommend Negro league candidates for the Hall just as white veterans were considered.

Over the years, nine Negro league stars have been chosen. The first was Satchel Paige. In August 1971, he was officially inducted at Cooperstown, New York. He said to the crowd, "I am the proudest man on the face of the earth today."

Others followed Paige: Josh Gibson, Buck Leonard, James "Cool Papa" Bell, Judy Johnson—Judy said to the gathering, "I am so grateful!"—Monte Irvin, Oscar Charleston, John Henry Lloyd, Ray Dandridge, and the Cuban ace Martin Dihigo. Rube Foster was also named to the Hall to honor his role as founder of the Negro leagues in 1921.

In 1972, all of baseball suffered a great loss when Jackie Robinson died at the age of fifty-three. His magnificent major league career had lasted only ten years. He made the Dodgers champions. Most of all, he fulfilled the hopes and dreams of his race. The "great experiment" was a great success. He was inducted into the Hall of Fame.

In his retirement, however, Jackie suffered from diabetes and other ailments. Many said he was simply worn out after his remarkable but difficult life. He had had the courage not to fight back, as Branch Rickey had hoped, but it had taken a toll. Americans, black and white, mourned him.

Almost every former Negro league player was asked about Robinson. To a man they felt he was a true hero.

"That man—the courage that he had," said Jack Marshall. "I don't think the word *ambassador* would fit. It'd have to be *lion*. He was a lion. He was a tiger.

"To take the treatment that he took. I don't think that I could have taken it. I don't know any other person who could have.

Especially the fellas I played with. Branch Rickey must have been a genius to look at that man's brain and see that he could go through what he did."

Satchel Paige agreed. "Jackie was a good choice. Jackie got it goin' alright, but before he died he looked like my grandpa. They made him suffer a lot. He never did get over it.

"I'll tell you what. I was the top man, but they couldn't 'a' booted me around like they did Jackie. I'll tell ya now I wouldn't 'a' took it. I'd felt I didn't have to take that to stay up there."

Chet Brewer added, "Jackie was an excellent choice because of his intelligence. That, put together with his ability, made him a natural."

Robinson's death made former Negro league players feel a little older themselves. By the 1970s, with their leagues gone for more than twenty years, they began getting sad phone calls telling them about a teammate who was very sick, or another who had died. Some old-timers were healthy and fit; others were saddled with ailments. They decided to make an effort to get together and commemorate what they had done.

Each year reunions were held in different parts of the country—Chicago, Los Angeles, Kansas City. Former players came alone or brought their wives. Sometimes they had picnics, sometimes formal dinners. Writers interviewed them. Video cameras recorded their words and memories. In 1979, the town of Ashland, Kentucky, began hosting an annual reunion. Some of the players even brought their old uniforms. Buck Leonard proudly wore his Homestead Grays jersey. It was made of heavy wool, and it looked as fresh and impressive as it had when he was wearing it and standing alongside Josh Gibson.

The stories and the laughter flowed. The former players would

Old pros. Long after their careers had ended, Negro league players got together to tell stories and remember the bad old days. In 1972 this group reunited in Chicago. Standing (left to right): Carter Wilson, Perry Hall, Ted "Double Duty" Radcliffe, Alex Radcliffe, Subby Byas, Cool Papa Bell, Jack Marshall. Middle row (left to right): Hannibal Cox, Sugar Cornelius, David Malarcher, Ted Page, Jelly Garner, Jew Baby Bennett. Front (left to right): Maurice Wiggins, Jimmie Crutchfield, Bobby Andersen, Clarence Jones.

shake their heads at how they lived on fifty cents a day meal money. Or how, when there was no meal money, they ate cold pork and beans out of a can, or sardines and crackers. How they slept in cramped spaces on crowded buses. How heavy their uniforms were when they were drenched with sweat and coated with dust. How an entire team would take a bath in a big kettle in a backyard.

Chet Brewer told a story about a team bus, a jalopy with bad seats, bad breaks, bad everything. "But we had a driver who was a genius. No matter what went wrong, he could fix it," Brewer said. Finally the bus broke down one time too many. The owner of the team, Brewer said, took out a gun. "I'm gonna kill that SOB!" he shouted. The players thought he meant the driver. Instead, Brewer said, he shot the bus in the radiator!

They even laughed about the racism. Everybody had a story, or a remark, or a nasty incident. Once, when a white player said he wasn't going back to the major leagues "until I beat these niggers," a black player who heard him said to his teammates, "Let's keep him here for the next two years."

Mostly they talked baseball. The games. The plays. Men who were now in their seventies and eighties would jump to their feet and show how a play was made. When they were younger, they were hard sliders and tough fighters. Now they were old men with brittle bones, gentle voices, and much, much pride.

Some of them brought photographs and newspaper clippings. A few former players made a hobby of researching and collecting data on the leagues. They researched exhibition games between Negro league players and white all-star teams. They loved to compare players and make up all-time all-star lineups. Some players brought entire scrapbooks.

These documents were important to them. Black baseball did not have the official scorekeepers and historians of major league baseball. There were no videotapes, no recordings of radio broadcasts. Black newspapers were the only real source of information aside from what the players themselves had collected and saved as they traveled. If they had a chance, that is. Often they were in another city when an article in a local newspaper appeared. Usually it was their wives who clipped articles and mounted team photographs on construction paper. Cool Papa Bell's wife, Clarabelle, kept good scrapbooks.

So did Jimmie Crutchfield.

"I was so small when I started playing that people constantly told me I was never going to make it," said Crutch. "I figured I had to keep a scrapbook right from the beginning just to show them. There's not one or two players with better books than mine. I get the books out once in a while. I can tell people who say, 'I never heard of you,' a lot of things. I wasn't just a run-of-the-mill ballplayer. I contributed something."

Mostly, the old-timers had their friendships. You don't ride nine hours on a bus seven days a week, they said, and not build friendships that last a lifetime. Just the chance to see old friends was enough to make them travel long distances to get to the reunions. They were "travelin' men," so this was nothing new. Cool Papa Bell said one year, "The doctor told me I was taking my life into my hands coming up here. But I said that I am a ballplayer first."

Almost always, the old-timers were asked two questions: "How do you compare your baseball with major league baseball?" and "Are you bitter that you were not able to play in the major leagues?"

How did they compare? Cool Papa Bell described it best.

"We played a different kind of baseball than the white teams. We played *tricky* baseball. We did things they didn't expect," Bell, one of the fastest and trickiest, said with a smile.

Many of the old-timers would nod and smile at this.

"We'd bunt and run in the first inning. Then when they would come in for a bunt we'd hit away. We always crossed them up," Bell said. "We'd run the bases hard and make the fielders throw too quick and make wild throws. We'd fake a steal home and rattle the pitcher into a balk."

As Bell talked other players jumped in. One said that when Bell was playing center field he would run all the way in behind second base and catch a pick-off throw from the pitcher.

Sometimes Cool Papa even stretched the rules.

"You had to watch him on the bases," said Jack Marshall. "I saw him go from first to third and he never even touched second. He ran inside it by three feet when the umpire wasn't looking!"

And were they bitter about not being permitted in the major leagues?

Almost always, they said no.

"No, I don't feel bitter," said Ted "Double Duty" Radcliffe. "You know how the world was in those days. The fact is, I come along too early. You can't change things. I had a nice career. I don't feel bitter."

Some were upset only about bad timing. The door opened when they were too old.

"I was very happy about Jackie Robinson," said Jimmie Crutchfield. "I knew that Jackie could make it. I was thirty-seven years of age [in 1947] and there were a lot of ballplayers, the best ballplayers that we had, and they had passed their peak. It was kind of tough to take. It was all over. It was too late for me."

Cool Papa Bell even had kind words about white owners who upheld the color line. "We had good white people, but they had to accept what the public accepts," Bell said. "People were afraid to speak out. A lot of white owners wanted to sign us, but they couldn't speak out."

Others looked back over their days in the Negro leagues and considered them the best times of their lives.

"They were my happy days," said Judy Johnson. "I enjoyed every minute of it. If I had to live it over again, I would go over it again. I think it was worth living. It taught you to be a man and a gentleman in every respect. It taught you how to treat your fellow man."

To a man they called themselves "lucky." Even with all the hardships, the traveling, days with two and three games in 100-degree heat, bad food, racism, and very little money, they considered themselves lucky.

Said Ted Page, "I'm one of the luckiest guys in the world. I'm lucky to be able to play with all those great ballplayers."

Jake Stevens, who for many years played shortstop for Hilldale in Philadelphia, said, "I've had the happiest life any man ever could."

Slowly, the years took more great names. Satchel Paige died in 1982 at the age of seventy-six, or thereabouts. Cool Papa Bell died in 1991. He was eighty-eight.

On June 26, 1993, Roy Campanella died at age sixty-nine. Campy was paralyzed from injuries he suffered in an auto accident in 1958 that ended his great baseball career. At age fifteen, Campanella had begun playing part-time with the Negro league Bacharach Giants in Philadelphia. Many years of black baseball later, he joined the major league Brooklyn Dodgers at age twenty-six. He went on to win *three* Most Valuable Player awards. And now he was dead. Another pioneer had passed on.

The Los Angeles Dodgers held a ceremony in Dodger Stadium to commemorate Campy's death. The scoreboard showed a courageous man in a wheelchair. But if Campy had been there, he would have wanted the fans to remember him as that strong-as-an-ox catcher for the Brooklyn Dodgers, and for the Baltimore Elite

Giants before that. Especially for the Elite Giants. He would have hoped that the young major league ballplayers, particularly those with black faces, would never forget the sweat and dust, the courage and dedication, the love of baseball by men who had to play a separate game.

Black baseball.

The Negro leagues.

BOX SCORE

Who was the best? Who was the greatest power hitter? Who threw the best fastball? Who was the best base-stealer? Who was the best-fielding shortstop? Which player was most valuable?

These are the questions all baseball fans love to throw at one another. Black baseball fans were no different. Who were the greatest Negro League stars?

Through black baseball's sixty-year history, many "dream teams" were put together by writers, fans, coaches, and players. Many of the same players appear on all the lists, but many great players performed so long ago that nobody alive today ever saw them. That makes it almost impossible to compare them with great players who came later.

But the all-time all-star teams are still fun to put together. What follows is a variety of teams put together by many different "experts."

SABR All-Stars

(All-Star team named in 1975 by Negro Leagues Research Committee of the Society for Baseball Research {SABR}. David Malarcher, who played in early 1900s, was a member of the committee. Malarcher did not vote for himself.)

RHP	SMOKEY JOE WILLIAMS *New York Lincoln Giants 1910–1932*
LHP	WILLIE FOSTER *Chicago American Giants 1923–1937*
C	BIZ MACKEY *Newark Eagles 1920–1948*
1B	BEN TAYLOR *Indianapolis ABC's 1911–1929*
2B	BINGO DEMOSS *Chicago American Giants 1915–1929*
3B	RAY DANDRIDGE *Newark Eagles 1933–1949* DAVID MALARCHER *Chicago American Giants 1916–1935*
SS	JOHN HENRY LLOYD *New York Lincoln Giants 1907–1931*
OF	OSCAR CHARLESTON *Pittsburgh Crawfords 1915–1939* CRISTOBEL TORRIENTI *Chicago American Giants 1913–1931* PETE HILL *Chicago American Giants 1904–1925*
UTILITY	MARTIN DIHIGO *Cuban Stars* WILLIE WELLS *St. Louis Stars* BULLET ROGAN *Kansas City Monarchs*

Greatest Teams

(Based on author's research and opinion of former players David Malarcher, Jimmie Crutchfield, and Jack Marshall)

NEW YORK CUBAN GIANTS 1906–1910

NEW YORK LINCOLN GIANTS 1911–1917

C. I. TAYLOR'S INDIANAPOLIS ABC's 1911–1919

RUBE FOSTER'S CHICAGO AMERICAN GIANTS 1910–1922

CUM POSEY'S HOMESTEAD GRAYS 1916–1934 1937–1945

GUS GREENLEE'S PITTSBURGH CRAWFORDS 1932–1936

Greatest Team of All Time

1936 Pittsburgh Crawfords

P   SATCHEL PAIGE, SAM STREETER, LEROY MATLOCK, HARRY "TINCAN" KINCANNON, THEOLIC "FIREBALL" SMITH, ERNEST "SPOON" CARTER

C   JOSH GIBSON, BILL PERKINS

1B   OSCAR CHARLESTON, JOHN WASHINGTON

2B   DICK SEAY

3B   JUDY JOHNSON

SS   CHESTER WILLIAMS

OF   JIMMIE CRUTCHFIELD, COOL PAPA BELL, SAM BANKHEAD, BILL PERKINS

Buck Leonard's All-Time Team

P	TEDDY TRENT, SATCHEL PAIGE, LEROY MATLOCK
C	JOSH GIBSON, BIZ MACKEY, BILL PERKINS
1B	BUCK LEONARD
2B	SAMMY T. HUGHES
3B	RAY DANDRIDGE, JUDY JOHNSON
SS	WILLIE WELLS
OF	VIC HARRIS, COOL PAPA BELL, TURKEY STEARNS, BILL WRIGHT
Utility	MARTIN DIHIGO

Normal "Tweed" Webb's All-Star Team

(Webb was a semi-professional player and Negro league historian.)

P	SATCHEL PAIGE, SMOKEY JOE WILLIAMS, BULLET JOE ROGAN, JOHN DONALDSON, WILLIE FOSTER
C	BIZ MACKEY
1B	BEN TAYLOR
2B	BINGO DEMOSS
3B	DAVID MALARCHER
SS	JOHN HENRY LLOYD
OF	OSCAR CHARLESTON, COOL PAPA BELL, MULE SUTTLES, CRISTOBEL TORRIENTI
Utility	VIC HARRIS, WILLIE WELLS
Manager	RUBE FOSTER

Team Selected by Claude Campbell of Washington, D.C., in 1946

(Campbell wrote articles under the name "The Spike Shoe.")

P	JOE WILLIAMS, DICK REDDING, DAVE BROWN
C	BIZ MACKEY, BRUCE PETWAY
1B	BEN TAYLOR
2B	SAMMY T. HUGHES
3B	BILL BLACKMON
SS	JOHN HENRY LLOYD
OF	CRISTOBEL TORRIENTI, OSCAR CHARLESTON, RAP DIXON, CHARLIE SMITH

Utility DICK LUNDY

Author's All-Time Nickname Team

TED "Double Duty" RADCLIFFE   JAMES "Cool Papa" BELL

WILLIE "The Devil" WELLS   TEDDY "Big Florida" TRENT

GEORGE "Georgia Rabbit" BALL   HARRY "Tincan" KINCANNON

ARTHUR "Rats" HENDERSON   ERNEST "Spoon" CARTER

L.D. "Goo Goo" LIVINGSTON   ROBERT "Highpockets" HUDSPETH

CARROLL "Dink" MOTHEL

NORMAN "Turkey" STEARNS   OLIVER "Ghost" MARCELLE

FRANK "Groundhog" THOMPSON   GEORGE "Mule" SUTTLES

Cool Papa Bell's All-Star Team

P   SMOKEY JOE WILLIAMS, SATCHEL PAIGE, BULLET JOE ROGAN, BILL HOLLAND

C   BIZ MACKEY, JOSH GIBSON, BRUCE PETWAY, LARRY BROWN

1B   BUCK LEONARD

2B   SAMMY T. HUGHES, BINGO DeMOSS

3B   JUDY JOHNSON

SS   WILLIE WELLS, JOHN HENRY LLOYD

OF   JUD WILSON, TURKEY STEARNS, OSCAR CHARLESTON, COOL PAPA BELL, JIMMIE CRUTCHFIELD

BIBLIOGRAPHY

Alvarez, Mark. *The Official Baseball Hall of Fame Story of Jackie Robinson*. New York: Simon and Schuster, 1990.

Ashe, Arthur. *A Hard Road to Glory: A History of the African American Athlete*. New York: Warner Books, 1988.

Brashler, William E. *Josh Gibson: A Life in the Negro Leagues*. New York: Harper & Row, 1978.

Bruce, Janet. *The Kansas City Monarchs: Champions of Black Baseball*. Lawrence: University of Kansas Press, 1985.

Chadwick, Bruce. *When the Game Was Black and White*. New York: Abbeville Press, 1992.

Couzens, Gerald Secor. *A Baseball Album*. New York: Lippincott & Crowell, 1980.

Craft, David. *The Negro Leagues*. New York: Crescent Books, 1993.

Dixon, Phil, with Patrick J. Hannigan. *The Negro Baseball Leagues: A Photographic History*. Mattituck, N.Y.: Amereon House, 1992.

Holway, John B. *Voices from the Great Black Baseball Leagues*. New York: Dodd, Mead & Company, 1975.
————. *Black Diamonds: Life in the Negro Leagues from the Men Who Lived It*. New York: Stadium Books, 1991.

Humphrey, Kathryn Long. *Satchel Paige*. New York: Franklin Watts, 1988.

Kahn, Roger. *The Boys of Summer*. New York: Harper & Row, 1971.

Okrent, Daniel, and Harris Lewine. *The Ultimate Baseball Book*. Boston: Houghton Mifflin, 1979.

Peterson, Robert B. *Only the Ball Was White*. Englewood Cliffs, N.J.: Prentice-Hall, 1970.

Rogosin, Donn. *Invisible Men: Life in Baseball's Negro Leagues*. New York: Atheneum, 1983.

Smith, Robert. *Pioneers of Baseball*. Boston: Little, Brown, 1978.

Tygiel, Jules. *Baseball's Great Experiment: Jackie Robinson and His Legacy*. New York: Oxford University Press, 1983.

Veeck, Bill. *Veeck as in Wreck: The Autobiography of Bill Veeck*. New York: Fireside, 1989.

Photography Credits: Bill Brashler: pp. 3, 18, 27, 32, 35, 48, 51, 54, 61, 64, 68, 71, 90, 92, 93, 98, 103, 108, 126, 132, 136, 142, 149; Chicago Tribune: pp. 16, 63, 89; William Price Fox: p. 129; Dr. Lawrence Hogan: pp. ii (frontispiece), 14, 30, 44, 113, 131, 138; Jerome Holtzman: p. 41; Refocus Productions: p. 28; Ken Solarz: pp. 12, 21, 70, 91; Mary-Frances Veeck: pp. 77, 140.

INDEX

Page numbers in italic type refer to photo captions.